THE THIRD EYE DIET

THE
THIRD
EYE
DIET

Intuition Nutrition
for Spiritual Activation

ALYSSA MALEHORN

LIONCREST
PUBLISHING

THE THIRD EYE DIET
Intuition Nutrition for Spiritual Activation

ISBN   978-1-5445-1928-9 *Hardcover*
       978-1-5445-1927-2 *Paperback*
       978-1-5445-1926-5 *Ebook*

For Wolf and Zack, in order of appearance.

CONTENTS

INTRODUCTION

Think of someone you deeply admire, not just for what they've accomplished but for who they are as a person. A person who seems at home in their body, who seems to react with grace to every situation. A person who seems to know the energy in the room as soon as they walk into it. Guided by their intuition, they move through life with effortless confidence, seeing the potential for good in everything that happens around them. They are like a great musician, and the world is their instrument.

When you're around this person, you instantly feel at ease, grounded. Their presence puts your problems and uncertainties to rest. Being around them, you just *feel* better.

But even though you may have often tried to emulate their confidence in your own life—to think and act in a way that channels the balance and beauty they project—it's proved to be challenging for you. It's as though they have something extraordinary. Something supernatural. And you might even have felt like you'd give anything to learn the secret knowledge they seem to have.

You may have spent years trying one spiritual practice after another in hopes that it will boost you up to that higher self that this person embodies. But the more teachings or practices you collect, the less connected you may feel to yourself. Even the blissed out spiritual high that comes from intensive energy work can leave you feeling spacey and disconnected. Meanwhile, when you do make progress, it doesn't seem to stick.

In contrast, this person seems entirely grounded. Their energy isn't manufactured—it's completely natural. They have embodied their highest self. They're in their true, divine nature.

"YOU'RE SO SENSITIVE"

In your life, you may have been labeled "sensitive" often enough to know it's not always a compliment. It's a word that sometimes gets used for people who can't take a joke, who always perceive themselves as being slighted, who react to every small setback as if it is a full-blown crisis.

At times, your sensitivity has likely served you well, alerting you to potential danger or guiding you to take necessary action. But sometimes your sensitivity may make you feel like an outsider. When you try to ignore it, to just be like everyone else, you may regret not listening to your intuition. But when you let your sensitivity run your life, it can leave you feeling fragile, exposed, alone.

If that's where you find yourself, your level of sensitivity is working against you, not for you.

When we act, think, or sense from this level of instability (with accompanying emotions like fear, control, or anger), we experience what the energy healing world refers to as "constriction." There's a reason you can feel tightness in your body during moments of fear—maybe your throat closes up when you're engaged in an argument, or your stomach clenches into a ball when you're anxious. If this is your experience, you're far from alone. Living in an energetically constricted state is a cultural epidemic in this day and age.

The constricted self, also called the "lower self," is primarily oriented toward survival. When you are living mainly through the lower self, your energy or "lightbody" is unable to function at a higher level. In that constricted state, every effort toward spiritual growth can feel like pushing a boulder up a hill. Your body saves its energy for only the most necessary, survival-oriented tasks.

However, as you move out of this constricted state, your sensitivity actually becomes a support system. Over time, it changes from a liability to a superpower.

Think of it this way: if you have a highly refined sense of smell, you're going to enjoy a walk through a rose garden a lot more than most people. However, you're also going to be more alert to the smell of strong cologne or road fumes. Similarly, a heightened spiritual sensitivity allows you to tune in to both high and low vibrational states. Learning to focus more attention on the high vibe state paves the way for natural expansion, the opposite of constriction. In a state of expansion, your body and mind become more open, more receptive, which leads to the awakening of your natural intuitive gifts.

The key is making the choice as to how you want to live, constricted or expanded, and finding ways to support that state of being.

And that's what this book is all about!

Almost no one lives 100 percent of the time in either the lower self or higher self. Rather, we all tend to ping-pong between both until we've more fully integrated the higher self, the aspect of us that lives beyond the limitations of fear. The important thing to remember is that living from within the higher self is not limited to a chosen few. Rather, it's the most natural state for you (and everyone) to live in. After all, if humans were built to live from the lower self, it would be health-promoting. But instead, operating in a near-constant state of constriction is completely degenerative to every system in our body. No wonder chronic illness is such a widespread issue today!

TRUSTING YOURSELF

You've probably come to this book because you're not feeling as connected with your true self as you'd like to be. You may have trouble trusting your inner voice, and that lack of trust may have led you into some challenging situations. You may feel really sensitive and may be trying to get a handle on those feelings and how you respond to them.

If that's where you find yourself, I'm so excited to welcome you to this journey. For the past twenty-five years, it's been my joy to partner with lightworkers and old souls just like you, who are ready to shift into a higher level of spiritual consciousness and unlock the gifts they were put on earth to offer.

If you're unfamiliar with these terms, that's okay. Believe it or not, they likely describe *you*!

A lightworker is anyone who feels the desire to be in service to others and/or the planet. They have a healer's heart and know that they are part of something bigger than themselves. They often gravitate toward the healing arts but can be found in every walk of life and every career imaginable. Lightworkers are driven to answer the call of their soul and are committed to living beyond the limitations of fear.

An old soul is someone who, having lived many lifetimes, has progressed through the first several stages of soul development (infant, child, adolescent, mature) and is now operating from a more heart-centered state. Old souls typically can feel overwhelmed by modern life—they might feel like they're the "black sheep" of their family of origin or feel out of place with their culture. Because their healing nature can be felt a mile away, old souls tend to have their own emotional issues and traumas to heal, as well as attract other people who are struggling with issues and need a soft place to land. They may often compromise themselves for the benefit of others until they learn a new way of being. Waking up to who they really are helps them attract other old souls and step into their true power.

For more details, see my book *How Old Is Your Soul? The Essential Guide to the Lessons, Gifts and Archetypes of Every Soul Age.*

The *Third Eye Diet* is all about rediscovering your truly natural state and retraining yourself to live from it by elevating consciousness via third eye activation. As you reclaim your innate spiritual gifts, your sensitivity will become your friend, even if it has felt like a curse in the past. You'll know when to constrict and when to expand. You'll be able to truly trust your body, your mind, and your emotions. You'll be able to make correct discernments about what you're sensing—in other words, to operate confidently out of your intuition.

As you get started on this journey, I want to reassure you that *you already have everything that you need* to experience the connection you desire. You are naturally wired to live from and through your highest self, to operate in perfect flow with your intuition, and to naturally feel connected with all other living things.

As a side note, this book has the potential to create a coherent state within you as you read. It's energetically encoded with coherent frequencies to support you in shifting to your next level. The words themselves have encoded frequencies designed to elevate your perception and coherence. Just by reading the words on this page, the words themselves are triggers to activate the higher vibrational templates that already exist within you.

You can meet that energy by releasing any resistance you have to your own expansion and elevation. The key is making a conscious choice to receive these words and the ideas they express, and to let the processes unfold beyond your intellect. As you read this, put yourself in a place of willingness to receive higher-level wisdom and release whatever doesn't apply.

Immerse yourself in the energy of the book rather than holding it at arm's length until you intellectually grasp it.

To expand out of that lower self, all you have to do is take steps toward activating what's naturally within you. In doing so, you'll start to access higher levels of an inner knowing. With this knowing comes peace, clarity, and an ability to understand life's situations through a higher-level awareness. This increases flow in every part of your life.

Instead of being overwhelmed by challenges, you'll be empowered to honor and learn from every situation you're in.

Instead of buying into the stories that are triggered by stress and can lead you down the rabbit hole of worry, confusion, and chaos, you'll be able to access a higher-level perspective that lets you experience power, clarity, and love.

Instead of fighting against your limits to get what you want out of life, you'll experience a limitless state of being, where everything you sense helps you get what you want—and more importantly, be who you're meant to be.

It's an incredible joy, and I'm so excited for you to experience it.

Wondering what all this has to do with your diet? Turn the page to find out.

CHAPTER 1

WHAT I MEAN
BY "DIET"

Like a lot of people, I spent the early part of my life seeing "diet" as a four-letter word, one that (not coincidentally) had the word "die" in it. The word signified restriction, punishment, willpower. Nevertheless, I spent most of my early twenties jumping from one restrictive eating regimen to another.

If you'd met me then, you'd probably never have guessed how much what I ate distracted me. I lived a life dedicated to healing—not only as a natural psychic medium, intuitive channel, and energy healer, but at the time, I was also a massage therapist and a Reiki master teacher. But like so many people, I focused on food as a means to survive and (I hoped) eventually thrive. My specific goals for dieting varied from eating all the "right" things while I was pregnant with my son to losing the weight after his birth to improving my dissatisfaction with how I looked and felt physically. But all these goals had a common denominator: seeing my physical body as a burden. I was in a cycle of self-criticism, setting unrealistic goals for my body and judging it harshly if I didn't reach or maintain those results.

What kept me from realizing the negative effects of that distraction was the belief that this one diet (whatever it happened to be at the time) was going to finally set me free. Once I found the right food fix—whether it was a three-day cleanse or a six-month reset—my body would be on auto-pilot after that. Between now and then, life might be super challenging, but it would all be worth it. Crossing that finish line, I believed, would allow me to relax and finally begin living the way I really wanted to: free. No matter what I was in search of at the time—less inflammation, more energy, a certain number on the scale, or just a lighter, cleaner feeling—I believed the only way to get it was by denying myself what I wanted. In a word: sacrifice.

If that seems like contradictory thinking to you, you're right.

DIET DEFINITIONS

You might be wondering why I'm using the word "diet" in a book about spirituality. The reason is that your diet is so much more than the food you eat.

"Diet" first appeared in English in the thirteenth century. From its origins, the word referred to "habitually taken food and drink." In the middle and early modern English periods, "diet" was used in another sense, to mean "way of living." The word's Greek ancestor is *diatia*, which is derived from a long verb meaning "to lead one's life." This included not just what was ingested but what type of work was done, how long the day was, and how long one slept.

In the classical sense, "diet" refers to our habitual nourishment—the things that we regularly turn to when our resources are depleted and we need to be "refilled." While this certainly applies to our physical bodies and what we eat and drink, it also applies to the emotional, mental, and spiritual bodies. Things like the route that you habitually drive, the media that you habitually consume, the relationships you take part in, what you consider to be self-care, and your general outlook on life.

All of that history around the word points to an important truth: just as your body has to process, filter, and integrate the food and drink you consume, it has to do the same work with everything else you consume. You are what you eat but also what you see, smell, touch, listen to, and think about.

We are always becoming what we consume. For example, if you frequently watch a TV show in which people fight all the time, you may start to notice yourself becoming more argumentative. If you spend a lot of time with a friend who complains constantly, you become more likely to complain. This usually begins in an unconscious way, meaning that we don't notice we're doing it—until we wake up to it.

In today's health-focused culture, it's common for people to get obsessed with the cleanliness of what they eat and drink. However, few people take the time to similarly assess the other things they consume. They unconsciously graze on what's being fed to them, whatever's popular or available, from TV shows to news to their social community. As a result, they unknowingly expose themselves to things that can damage their overall well-being and disrupt their spiritual journey with psychic interference that scrambles the clear signal trying to come through from their highest selves.

What may surprise you is that this damage and disruption has less to do with the content of what you consume and more to do with how you consume it. Even the most seemingly healthy lifestyle can create unforeseen challenges if you're pursuing it in a way that constricts your state of flow.

Flow, or balanced movement, is the natural order of this universe. All is energy, and all energy is naturally in flow. When energies (emotions, communication, even physical fluids such as blood) cease to flow, constriction and stagnation occur, and problems (physical, mental, emotional, spiritual) are the result.

We've already talked briefly about constriction in the introduction. It's that sensation of tightness or desperation that comes from feeling threatened, triggered, or trapped. As you may have already perceived, the popular definition of "diet" is loaded with messaging that promotes constriction. You hear the word and immediately think of all the things you *can't* eat. That's exactly what makes it so difficult to stay on a diet! Constriction can't coexist with flow, and the constrictive effect of focusing on what you can't eat makes it impossible for you to enjoy what you can eat. Even if you do lose weight or improve your physical health, when feeling restricted, it's a challenge to allow the feelings of happiness, connection, or spiritual bliss.

MY DIET

It's no coincidence that "low" was the word that linked all the different food regimens I tried: low calorie, low carb, low fat. Each experiment in restrictive eating left me with lower vibrational patterns that impacted both my personal happiness and my work as a healer.

What does that look like? I became more self-critical and less patient with myself. I wasn't holding boundaries with my time and energy and felt chronically overwhelmed with life in general.

But starting in my late twenties and extending into my early thirties, the focus of my dieting changed. No longer was it about losing weight and looking good. Instead, my restrictive approach to eating was an effort to heal the mysterious illnesses that were slowly taking over my life. I kept changing my habits, putting new foods on the "Don't Touch" list in an effort to outrun one allergic reaction or sensitivity after another.

Before long, it wasn't only food that was causing these reactions. My body was triggered by perfumes, cleaning products, home furnishings, tap water, even by things I saw on TV. This was my first clue that "diet" was a lot more than just food.

I tried for years to shrug off my symptoms (fatigue, lethargy, muscle pain, joint pain, adrenal fatigue, migraines) as the result of working too much or undergoing serious challenges in my life at that time. Telling myself it would get better eventually, I tried to push through the pain. But it didn't get better. Without any apparent rhyme or reason, I had heart palpitations, nervous system issues, and felt sharp pains traveling from one part of my body to another, as my kidneys and liver struggled to handle my body's toxic load.

Once it got bad enough, I stopped trying to fix the symptoms myself and began visiting doctors. More than twenty, in fact. Most of them put my symptoms down to autoimmune diseases like chronic fatigue or fibromyalgia. Some even told me it was all in my head.

Finally, one doctor diagnosed me with dysautonomia, which is essentially the malfunction of the autonomic nervous system, arising in my case from multiple chemical sensitivities.

This diagnosis confirmed my growing belief about the definition of "diet." Eating all the perfect foods couldn't balance out the effects of other things I was consuming through smell, sight, and sound: energy. As I began to pay more attention to the things in my environment that triggered reactions, I became more attuned to the immaterial factors affecting me, as well.

For the first time, I saw that my "diet" even included my relationships, my spiritual practices, what I thought about, how I perceived the challenges in my life at the time and in my past. In short, every aspect of how I lived my life.

This opened my eyes to see that hyperfocusing on the physical had been siphoning energy from my emotional, mental, and spiritual reserves. I'd unwittingly adopted and accepted a fragmented lifestyle, living as though each part of me was separate from the others. As a result, I felt depleted and overwhelmed in every area of my life.

That finally led me to the biggest realization: that almost all of my actions were unconsciously fear-based. Most everything I was doing at that time was done with a conscious focus on love, but I was *un*consciously focusing on avoiding death from those health issues. This fear-based energy was creating incredible constriction and inner conflict within me. As a result, even though I wasn't actually physically dying, I certainly wasn't actively healing either.

This realization produced an awakening moment that

changed my life. I saw that I had to make the shift from making choices based on fear to making choices based on love. My love of being here on this magnificent earth, my love for my son and for the gift I had to be his parent, my love of life and being in service to others, my love for my physical body and how strong it had been through all the turmoil it was experiencing.

I can't overstate how significant that shift was for me. It allowed me to see the deeper truth behind all my previous realizations: that diet is much more than just nutrition that we absorb in our physical bodies. I'd seen for myself that even eating all of the "perfect" healing foods did no good if I was tangled in a self-imposed web of stress, anxiety, and perfectionism. If I wanted to be fully well again, I had to start by addressing the constriction that had been quietly siphoning my energies all this time.

CONSTRICTION AND CONDITIONING

That phase of my life demonstrates how constriction dramatically affects the way we process, filter, and integrate everything we consume, from food to emotions to information. But how does constriction show up in the first place?

For most of us, constriction subtly creeps in through conditioning—the habits and beliefs we absorb through the culture and environment that surround us. Some of this is easy to trace, but the most influential conditioning in your life is usually subconscious, implanted there without your consent or awareness, through significant events with a high emotional volume or long-term experiences of disharmony or low-level anxiety. Even if you have consciously renounced those types of beliefs and habits, they can still powerfully influence what you consume and how.

I grew up deeply immersed in a religious culture that conditioned me to live under the influence of fear. As a child, I sensed things that I couldn't understand, such as the presence of beings in spirit (including ghosts and other entities) in our dark hallway. With no way to understand those things, I felt confused, powerless, and scared nearly all the time. The only way my child self knew to deal with that level of stress was to normalize it—my body and mind learned to live in a state of constant low-level anxiety (constriction). But making it normal didn't make it good or beneficial for me. As time went on, that "diet" of fear altered the makeup of my entire body.

My religious background also conditioned me to believe that martyrdom was a virtue. Throughout time, many religions have spread the message that love, forgiveness, and transcendence must be earned through suffering and sacrifice. This belief was emphasized as I grew up and learned the "No pain, no gain" mantra that society uses to glorify struggle. From workouts to professional goals to personal growth, most of us begin to believe that our achievements aren't valid unless they're the result of blood, sweat, and tears. Thanks to this conditioning, I was fully convinced that I could only feel good when I was working ridiculously hard and that the more I suffered and deprived myself, the more free and whole I'd eventually feel.

Fueled by this conditioning, I became an expert at living in survival mode, to the point where nobody (including myself) realized how much I was struggling. From the outside, it looked as though I thrived under pressure. In reality, I was using so much unconscious energy to simply survive that I delayed waking up the conscious aspects of myself that could have allowed me to be a compassionate witness to myself. That witness mode would have paved the way for shifting out of survival into thriving.

WHAT IS NATURAL FOR YOU?

Shifting out of constriction starts with learning to recognize what feels natural for *you*. As soon as you become aware of the conditioning that is driving you, you can discern how it motivates your habits, especially what you habitually consume.

As you grow in your perception of what feels natural for you, you'll also become aware that the freedom you're after isn't actually about losing weight, looking better, or even feeling better. What you may not know that you're really seeking is a sense of unity between the conscious self and unconscious self that allows those aspects to work together, as they're designed to.

But until that unity happens, your instinct is most likely to seek a sense of stability and safety through family, culture, or community. Much of our unconscious conditioning carries a huge emotional weight, and the instinctive way to counterbalance that weight is through relationships. All humans crave a sense of belonging; it's a desire embedded deeply in our DNA. In the ancient world, those who strayed from the pack were much less likely to survive. By clinging closely to our tribes, we feel safe, protected, whole.

That's why you may find yourself unconsciously mimicking

the patterns exemplified by the people within your tribe, from the food you eat to the media you consume to the conversations you have. To shore up this sense of belonging, we tend to reflexively conceal or apologize for our differences from the tribe as we spiritually grow and expand in consciousness.

This behavior is instinctive, a habit based out of an ancient survival mechanism. But the more conscious you become of your own conditioning, the more you can make conscious choices that support you in thriving as your true, unified, expanded self.

The food aspect of diet can be very helpful in understanding this better. As a child, you were probably taught to eat whatever was in front of you. If you were in a home where you were fed and didn't go hungry, the tastes of your childhood, the sensation of eating, and the feeling of fullness became associated with comfort. In adulthood, when you move out of your childhood home and start buying your own food, you have a chance to move away from your original conditioning and make conscious choices about how you eat. But for many people, the uncertainty and even anxiety associated with life in transition will drive them to seek out the comfort of conditioned eating habits.

Even as we become more accustomed to adulthood, we still likely follow some of that original conditioning around food. Instead of making conscious choices about what we eat or crave, we tend to follow the eating habits of others in our tribe. Eating the way they eat helps us fit in and makes it easy to share resources and even conversation. (Have you ever noticed how much people talk with each other about food?)

All of this can support you feeling safer and more secure

within your tribe. But have you ever thought about whether it makes you feel healthier, more stable, and whole within yourself? If it doesn't or you're not sure, then there may be constriction present in your energy system, counteracting your efforts to achieve higher consciousness. In other words, your true nature may not be fully aligned with the thoughts, beliefs, and foods of your family of origin or current tribe. That inner conflict between "this is just what we do" and the unknown is the constriction that we're talking about.

There's nothing wrong with adhering to any specific habitual choices. But remember that it's the unacknowledged patterns that tend to cause issues. Once you become aware of a habit or pattern, and then make a conscious choice, you automatically begin the healing process and are naturally moving into freedom.

BECOMING WHOLE

For me, understanding the true definition of diet came as an epiphany. I saw that no matter how many supplements I tried or how many healthy foods I ate, focusing only on the food aspect of my diet wasn't going to manifest the complete healing I was looking for.

This realization was pressed home, day after day, by a strong intuitive message urging me to *let go*. Most of us share the fear of losing control, and I was alive partly because I had tightly monitored my diet and reactions to chemicals. But the more I tuned into my higher self, the more I realized the innate power of intention. I didn't need to abandon my healthy lifestyle; rather, I was ready to approach those habits with expansion, love, and gratitude. I was learning the difference between an intention not to die and an intention to live.

It's only natural to focus primarily on the physical aspect of your being when you're experiencing physical symptoms of an undiagnosed illness. But hyperfocusing on one aspect of your life (especially when that aspect is the material/physical three-dimensional world) makes it nearly impossible to achieve unity between the multidimensional aspects of the conscious and the unconscious. Even if your body would benefit from healthier habits, it's important to know that changing one part of your life is a stepping stone—not the be-all-end-all. And if your efforts to improve your physical body are interwoven with stress and perfectionism, that constriction inevitably will have a sabotaging effect.

In our multidimensional world, we each have a physical body vehicle to care for within a specific environment. This vehicle is designed to support every other aspect of life. If I spend eight hours a day meditating but fail to take care of my physical body's other needs, my lifestyle is no healthier than someone who eats cookies all day and never takes time to meditate. Humans are multidimensional, multifaceted beings, and each aspect of our human experience is meant to nourish and support the whole. If you're awakening spiritually, if you relax into the process, you'll begin to notice the different aspects of your life and how they relate and support each other. That noticing yields the next step: making conscious choices that bring a unified harmony to your whole being.

CHALLENGES AND SHIFTS

Reading this book means you've reached an exciting point in your spiritual journey. You're waking up to yourself by bringing previously repressed, unconscious conditioning into your conscious mind. As you move through this book, you're going to confront yourself about *why* you think what you think and feel what you feel. You're going to discover which of your beliefs actually resonate with you and which you have unwittingly soaked up.

You're going to look at how you're taking care of yourself and know what to do to upgrade to the next level. Intuitive spiritual activation is underway!

Fortunately, the physical world is full of tools to guide and support your spiritual expansion. The first step is to examine the places where you're inhibiting that expansion. Remember, expansion and constriction do not coexist. When you approach spiritual enlightenment from a place of self-judgment, the result is typically stagnation or feeling like you're going around in circles.

That's why, as you move forward activating your natural higher consciousness, it's important to prepare yourself for the challenges you could encounter.

- First of all, not everyone around you will be experiencing awareness and awakening at the same time or at the same rate. Sometimes, this may lead to feeling like you're on your own.
- When you move deeply through your own spiritual awakening/activation process, you'll start to notice how every constriction and judgment you place on yourself is hindering your own expansive peace, freedom, relaxation, and love. Your job is to confront yourself and your beliefs at every turn, until you meet yourself habitually with unconditional love. Every. Single. Time.

- One of the most common fears people have in this process is the fear of losing themselves or losing "who they are." The truth is, you are losing who you *thought* you were to make way for who you truly are.

- As we open up and expand spiritually, many of us experience various activation/ascension "symptoms," which may include visual disturbances or hearing things. Dream states become enlivened. Body buzzing or electrical-type shocks are common. The physical body starts to move energy differently as we receive the light codes from the higher dimensions.

- As this process continues, we see ourselves and others through a lens of expanded consciousness, which can sometimes feel disorienting. Relationships can shift and sometimes hit unstable phases as our perspective elevates and the primary focus is taken from what's happening in the material world to what's happening within us, spiritually and emotionally. *Emotional healing and spiritual activation go hand in hand, and that changes relationships.*

We'll talk in more detail about these challenges, and how to handle them, in upcoming chapters. But for now, as you encounter these shifts, let the following encouragements give you hope and some practical guidance:

- First of all, know that *you are safe* even though you may feel occasional instability. You are, in effect, losing your mind—in the sense that you are losing the old conditioning that used to dictate your thoughts and feelings. What you're going through is normal in the process of spiritual ascension.

- Worrying about something does not keep you safe; this

is yet another example of conditioning. According to the universal spiritual law of attraction, when you worry about something, you're investing in the very outcome you fear. An important step in the path of spiritual awakening is learning how to efficiently use your *chi*, or life force, and worry is a draining, inefficient energy pattern.

Trust me, I know how weirdly comforting worry can feel. If you grew up around habitual fear and anxiety, worry feels familiar. When I was breaking out of the familial pattern of worry, I felt irresponsible and negligent when I wasn't worried. I thought that if I worried about someone, that meant I loved them. But love and worry are *not* the same thing; they're not even close on the vibrational scale. As you move through this book, releasing habitual anxiety and worry will become easier and easier—don't worry about it. (Haha!)

- You'll also likely find that you start to break away from groupthink (consciousness). At first, you might feel isolated from friends and family as you expand beyond who you've been in the past and tune into what feels right for *you now*. Know that you're not alone on this journey. Even as you're awakening your own self-authority, you're simultaneously remembering your natural state of overall unity/connectedness with all other living beings.

It's partly because of this challenge that we created the online gathering place called the Raw Spirituality Community. It's a warm, welcoming place where you're surrounded and supported by others on the same awakening journey. You're invited to explore our community at RawSpirituality.com.

- Contrary to the "no pain, no gain" message I believed in the past, the journey to higher spiritual consciousness is one that actually gets easier as you go along. (Thank goodness, right?) The more you develop spiritually, the less tolerance you have for the inner chaos and conflict that comes from being out of alignment with your true nature. Constriction becomes so uncomfortable that correcting it becomes as natural as pulling your hand away from a fire. The rules and restrictions around diet are no longer necessary once you're living in the flow of an expanded, unified state.
- Finally, know that as you start to expand your awareness, you'll find yourself experiencing multiple awakenings. At the beginning, these awakenings may be small or large in experience. At times, ascension can be destabilizing since you are shifting longstanding patterns. My goal with this book is to support you in moving through these elevations/awakenings. As you become familiar with how these phases feel, you'll find it easier and more natural to feel grounded and anchored in light with each upgrade you experience.

THE ESSENCE

Your diet is so much more than the food you eat. It's how you process, filter, and integrate everything you take in, from food to media, environment to relationships. Each of these elements is like a spoke on a wheel, pushing the whole forward by drawing it in toward the center. For you, the "center" is the goal that drew you toward this book in the first place.

Maybe you think of it as raising your awareness, connecting with your highest self, or activating your next level of intuition. All of these are intertwined—they are just different expressions of the natural process of spiritual awakening.

As you explore these various aspects of your diet, I want to emphasize that there are no right or wrong choices. It's impossible for you to make a mistake. While I'll be making suggestions based on my experience and that of students I've guided through this process, that doesn't mean my choices were good or bad or right or wrong.

You're reading this book because on some level, you're ready to make a change, to let go of what's holding you back, even if you don't know exactly what this is yet. Unacknowledged conditioning leads to ways of being and thinking that keep you in a constricted state.

When we encounter resistance in the process of change, it's easy to give up, to think, "I guess I can't change this—it's just the way I am." This disempowered thought is designed to keep you in the territory of the victim archetype. In contrast, acknowledging the motivations behind your choices creates empowerment, enabling you to tune into the divinity within yourself. With practice, you'll start to see problems as challenges, then as experiences, then as adventures, until finally, they begin to feel like exciting experiments in new possibilities.

A lot of people attribute their physical adversities to genetics. But we know that genes are not the ultimate deciding factors when it comes to disease. If you're interested in diving deeper into the energetic roots of disease, a great place to start is with the work of Dr. Joe Dispenza. (See the Resources section at the end of this book for a few recommended titles to explore.)

The more your perspective shifts, the more you will naturally gravitate toward people, things, and experiences that support your new perspective. Ever since I expanded beyond my fear-based childhood program, I'm now naturally drawn toward a diet (in the fullest sense) that supports me physically, emotionally, mentally, and spiritually. More importantly, once I stopped relying on something in the physical world to fix any issues I had, I gradually stopped seeing myself or anyone else as being broken or needing to be fixed. Instead of trying to be perfect or tolerating/resenting things and situations that don't feel resonant, now it's easy to tune into what feels aligned and harmonious, and make conscious choices based on what feels like flow.

We all experience ups and downs along the way toward remembering our true divine nature. The more you embrace the process, the more your perspective shifts, and the more you'll know exactly how to support yourself along the way.

Taking this time to explore your choices around diet is the first step toward the unity that is higher consciousness. Even if your actual choices don't change, the shift happens when you become conscious of what lies beneath those choices. By acting consciously, you activate the divine awareness that has been inside you all along. An important aspect of this is awakening the third eye, which we'll discuss in the very next chapter.

CHAPTER 2

WHAT I MEAN
BY "THIRD EYE"

Why do we sometimes crave the comfort and familiarity of a traditional religion, even when it involves a
hierarchy and ancient ideas of human unworthiness and
spiritual deservedness?

It's because the unawakened human always seeks authority
outside of itself. Even in a modern era that celebrates freedom, autonomy, and equality, many people are still looking
for a guru to guide them through life.

The word "guru" loosely translates as "light shining into the
darkness," and that's exactly what many of us naturally desire.
Those who seek organized religion may do so because they
feel lost, unable to see clearly for themselves, and long to find
a culture or an organization whose spiritual leadership will
show them the way.

What many don't realize is that the guidance they seek is
already alive and well inside of all of us. A little pine cone–

shaped gland, located between the two hemispheres of the brain, is the seat of your very own inner guru.

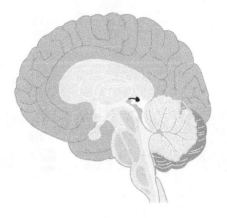

SAY HELLO TO YOUR PINEAL GLAND

You may have heard of the pineal gland referred to as the intuitive center, or the seat of the soul, because it's known to expand our awareness and perception of the world around and within us. It is the conductor for both physical and metaphysical perception, which is how it earned the name "the third eye."

On the physical plane, the pineal gland works with various parts of the brain, from the hypothalamus to the pituitary gland. Along with helping to balance the energy of the two sides of the brain and regulating certain hormones, your pineal gland acts as a light meter for your body. When light hits the sensitive nerve cells in your eye's retina, it activates the pineal gland to transmit information to the body about how to use that light.

But this isn't only true for visible light. The pineal gland also processes your response to what we could call spiritual light, i.e., higher levels of awareness and understanding of unity consciousness. When the pineal center is healthy, you're able to take more light into your body and fully process and integrate it.

Everything that happens in the physical realm has a matching etheric template—an energetic pattern that functions similarly to the physical process but on a metaphysical level. It might be best understood through the analogy of "phantom feelings," the phenomenon when people lose a limb but still feel that limb itch from time to time. You can even experience it for yourself by hovering your hand over your skin—that magnetic pull or tingle you feel is the energy of the etheric template.

Because of that etheric template, even someone who might have had their pineal gland removed will still experience energetic regulation, thanks to the energy center that still exists where the pineal gland used to be.

I know this from personal experience. Even though my thyroid gland was removed, my thyroid's energy center (also called the throat chakra) is alive and well. As a result of energy healing focused on that area, I'm able to express myself freely even without the physical gland being present.

For more in-depth exploration of the chakras and how they impact soul development, see my book *How Old Is Your Soul? The Essential Guide to the Lessons, Gifts and Archetypes of Every Soul Age.*

With your pineal gland sending light signals throughout your body, you feel awake and aware energetically. An even better way to put it is that you are literally enlightened—spiritually tuned in, your psychic abilities activated, your higher consciousness perceiving accurately. As a by-product, you feel more inclined to help other human beings and take care of the animal kingdom. Rather than a general sense of "me versus them," you tend to feel that there is a greater good shared by everyone and everything, beginning to more deeply understand that what's in your highest good is also in the highest good of all beings. There's a feeling of oneness within yourself and a sense of unity with the entire physical and spiritual world.

The pineal gland is also linked to the production of dimethyltryptamine, better known as DMT or "the God molecule." In recent years, we've seen a growing trend toward ingesting DMT and other hallucinogens in an attempt to activate higher levels of awareness. However, the truth is that our own brains are the only pharmacy we need to support our awakening.

Having a healthy pineal gland (third eye) means you can become the observer of your thoughts and proceed to make conscious choices about whether to align with them or not. When you act from a conscious place rather than conditioning, you might realize you've adopted certain thoughts because you've grown up with them, but you haven't stopped to think about whether they harmonize with you or your current lifestyle.

WHAT CALCIFICATION LOOKS LIKE

A healthy, "awakened" pineal gland facilitating higher states of awareness is the natural state for all sentient living beings who possess the gland. But when the gland becomes calcified, it depletes your body's production of melatonin and serotonin. This disrupts the circadian rhythm, affecting your sleeping/waking cycle, your seasonal cycle, and your mood.

A calcified pineal gland also means being less able to receive intuitive knowledge via spiritual light. It prevents you from having an open heart and mind, resulting in an impaired ability to observe life from a higher perception. A calcified pineal gland disrupts your sense of connection with your highest self, your spiritual source, and your intuition. With your perception impaired, you may feel fragmented, separate, or chronically in survival mode. As a result, you may perceive life as a zero-sum game—any benefit to you seems to impose a cost to others. By the same token, you may feel love and responsibility as a burden—a belief that if others are to benefit, it must feel like a sacrifice to you.

I've worked with many old soul clients over the years who made excuses for partners who abused them psychologically, emotionally, or physically: "He really does love me; he just has such deep, unresolved emotional wounds that he doesn't know how to show it." But once these clients began to decalcify their pineal gland, they awoke to the higher truth that they were not responsible for their partner's behavior. They could recognize their partner's challenges and offer support, but in an upgraded way, no longer sacrificing themselves for someone else's benefit.

To achieve that clarity, we need to take a few steps back and consider the stories that the unconscious mind is telling you. Ask yourself what external factors you've linked to your own value, worth, safety, or stability, and whether those links are true.

- Have you prioritized other's peace of mind over your own?
- Are you in the habit of making sure everyone else is okay, while not tuning in to your own needs?
- Do you walk on eggshells to limit other's potential reactions?

These behaviors indicate an unconscious conditioning based on prioritization of the perceived external world over your internal world. As with any choice, doing this isn't categorically right or wrong, but it's certainly not sustainable.

Take a minute and consider what stories you may have told yourself to justify unconscious behavior:

- That you won't be loved if you're not agreeable?
- That you'll be alone if you speak your truth?

By putting distance between yourself and whatever the story is, you're creating a sense of freedom, an opening that enables your expansion to begin.

THE CAUSE OF CALCIFICATION

So what causes the pineal gland to calcify? The short answer is everything. Interestingly, that's the same answer to the question of what can decalcify the pineal gland? Everything you eat, watch, live within, and relate to, as well as all of your previous conditioning, contributes to or subtracts from the health and activation of your pineal gland.

The ability to wake up to your own conditioning lives within your pineal gland. Decalcifying your pineal gland is a process that supports letting go of the ideas or beliefs that aren't natural to you. As the pineal gland decalcifies and the third eye energy center becomes healthier, you experience those beautiful aha moments that wake you up to the ways in which your conditioning doesn't resonate with your true self. Slowly but surely, you release constriction and achieve expansion. You start to emerge from thinking that you *are* your feelings and wake up the compassionate witness within.

Before I learned and integrated this, I used to be a pretty big control freak. Everything had to be a certain way for me to feel comfortable and safe, which was understandable considering my past health crises and psychic trauma. But as I moved through my decalcification process, my mind opened up to a world of possibilities. Suddenly, my way wasn't the only way anymore. I stopped believing that I had to have ownership of everything in my life. The feeling of this gradual clarity was amazing—for the first time, I started to truly relax. I let go of the need to control everything and felt waves of relief from the constant pressure I had normalized.

It's an amazing state of relaxation, connectedness, and peace. And the best thing about it? Maintaining that state doesn't feel like work. Because of the years I've spent decalcifying my third eye, constriction feels deeply uncomfortable to me. If I do feel fear, pressure, or a loss of control, I have new habits in place to learn from the feelings, release them, and repair any damage to my energy body. These habits have served me wonderfully over the years, and I'll guide you through them one by one in upcoming chapters.

AWAKE = EMPOWERED

Amazing things happen when humans are fully awake and

spiritually empowered. We no longer need to feed the military/industrial/pharmaceutical/agricultural control complex. Instead of killing animals and blocking off borders, we focus on taking care of one another. Our hearts are open to recognize others as divine beings. When we channel our energy into each other, that's when real change can happen. That's when we show up for another when they're in need. We allow ourselves to receive support when we need it. We break down the emotional heart-walls and open to true love for ourselves, humanity, and all beings.

This is reclaiming who we really are.

The military/industrial/pharmaceutical/agricultural complex, also known as MIPA, refers to the mutually financially beneficial relationships between governments, corporations, and organizations. These relationships are known to play a heavy hand in influencing public policy, but what many don't notice is how they work to normalize a lack of personal empowerment in the lives of everyday people.

Back in 1961, President Eisenhower actually warned the American people about what could happen if this complex was not carefully held in check:

> This conjunction of an immense military establishment and a large arms industry is new in the American experience. The total influence—economic, political, even spiritual—is felt in every city, every statehouse, every office of the federal government. We recognize the imperative need for this development. Yet we must not fail to comprehend its grave implications. Our toil, resources, and livelihood are all involved; so is the very structure of our society....

We must guard against the acquisition of unwarranted influence, whether sought or unsought, by the military-industrial complex. The potential for the disastrous rise of misplaced power exists, and will persist. We must never let the weight of this combination endanger our liberties or democratic processes....

Only an alert and knowledgeable citizenry can compel the proper meshing of the huge industrial and military machinery of defense with our peaceful methods and goals so that security and liberty may prosper together.[1]

At this stage in our history, the entire economic grid on this planet is based on a lack of empowerment. Some (though definitely not all) humans involved in the MIPA complex are filled with a level of complacency and sometimes even hatred for their fellow humans that makes no logical sense. Through decades of media-based brainwashing, we've been tricked into a fiercely loyal belief that our military, big corporations, pharmaceutical and agricultural industries have our best interest at heart.

Mind you, there's nothing inherently wrong with the military, big corporations, pharma or agricultural industries, nor with the humans who work in those fields. Most of the people involved in those industries are truly focused on being in service to others and the planet. There is, however, a darker agenda at work within this complex that must be illuminated to move beyond it into the light. This agenda involves a targeted effort to keep human beings in the dark. We are made to feel insecure and incoherent, anxious and depressed, with

---

1   "Military-Industrial Complex Speech, Dwight D. Eisenhower, 1961," Avalon Project, Yale Law School, https://avalon.law.yale.edu/20th_century/eisenhower001.asp.

a chronic baseline level of stress that keeps us in survival mode, never awakening to the truth of who we really are.

Today, our food and water supplies are completely toxified. In every resource we count on to sustain life as we know it—air, water, food, media, electromagnetic fields—there is some attempt to keep us asleep to our own empowerment through subtle messaging like the following:

- No one is their own guru. You must look to an authority figure for truth and direction.
- Perfection is unattainable, yet you must keep striving for it.
- You'll never be able to completely fix your food, water, the planet, not to mention all of your inner wiring.
- Greed is king. We're not our brother's keeper, so we each have to look out for number one.
- The MIPA complex is so powerful, there's nothing you can do to facilitate change. Keep trying or give up—it makes no difference.

It's a dark agenda, no question. But once you start to wake up to these forces and their messaging, you'll experience a snowball effect of consciousness expansion. Bit by bit, you'll notice where you can continue to support yourself and others, and you'll gain a sense of compassion for those going through the same awakening, as well as those who are still asleep. When we realize that those who are knowingly contributing to the self-limitation of others are themselves living in a deeply fearful energy body, that same compassion radiates through you to *all* beings—including those with an agenda based in fear.

DON'T BE DAUNTED

It's common for people at the beginning stages of awakening to feel a sense of grief for the time they've wasted. If that's how you feel now, let me assure you that you haven't lost anything, and everything happens in divine timing—no exceptions. You are exactly where you are meant to be at exactly the perfect time. Freedom is just around the corner. Every past situation, especially those of deep darkness or pain, offers spiritual benefit that will aid you in your awakening process. If it's hard to believe right now, that's okay—it will be clear soon. There is a part of you that already knows that beautiful things will come from challenging times. That part of you also already knows that you've always been free—you just weren't aware of it yet.

It's also common for people to feel a sense of overwhelm at all the "work" involved in spiritual expansion—so much conditioning to undo, so many new habits to learn. If that's how you feel now, think about it the way you would think about going on a long road trip. If you decided to drive from Florida to Canada and were determined to get there in just a few days, it would certainly feel overwhelming. But if you set out on your trip just intending to enjoy the ride—discovering new scenery, listening to music, having lots of time to think or converse with the person in the seat next to you—the trip would not only feel much more doable but would probably go by amazingly fast.

The Japanese word *Kaizen* refers to a series of small, continuous changes that might be unnoticeable on their own but eventually add up to big changes. In hypnotherapy, we often use the concept of *Kaizen* when someone wants to make a major lifestyle change. Let's say someone has been smoking a pack a day. Instead of quitting cold turkey, we might challenge them to work on smoking *almost* the entire pack, to just leave half an inch on the last cigarette and put it out. Two weeks later, they might start leaving an inch on the last cigarette. Then they'll work on leaving the entire cigarette unsmoked, and in the following weeks, they'll leave two, three, four. One day, they realize they've gone the whole day without any cigarettes, and it wasn't even that hard.

Studies show that the *Kaizen* method of slow, continuous change creates permanent change. People are less likely to slip back into old habits because their neurological systems have time to catch up to their behaviors. Some people are genetically wired to be able to handle big changes and fast adjustments, and that's great for them. However, if you know that you typically resist change, break it down. Make miniscule changes, as these are more likely to stick, and just keep going.

Remember, there's no prize for who awakens the quickest. You're not better or more advanced if you complete your spiritual awakening in a few months, a year, or even in this lifetime or never. The only requirement of this process is considering and addressing what's in front of you and within you right now. You don't even have to *know* what to do each day. You just have to start with one small agreement with yourself to begin to observe yourself and life differently, and be consistent with it.

THE ESSENCE

Every living being is already 100 percent empowered. We're just living in various stages of acknowledging that empowerment. We're naturally wired to have open hearts and feel spiritually connected to one another. Consider how babies act toward the world around them. When you were a baby, you couldn't have cared less about the color of anyone's skin, their religion, or their background. You didn't hesitate to cry out for what you needed or express how you felt. Over time, though, we develop layers of conditioning like a suit of armor, which creates physical and emotional rigidity. We become inflexible in our minds and physical bodies.

As you start to break down those layers in pursuit of expansion and empowerment, you'll realize that you're not grasping for something you never had. Think of this process as unwrapping the gift that's already inside of you. In doing so, you're releasing the rigidity and inflexibility and moving into *your soul's natural state of freedom.*

Many times, I've described the feeling of spiritual awakening as "coming home." I've frequently heard others express it in the same way. Clearly, there's a realization that somewhere along the journey, we may have felt as though we had abandoned or betrayed ourselves. Maybe you were in a relationship that wasn't honoring. Maybe you lived under the burden of perfectionism. Maybe you had a consistent pattern of judging others or yourself.

Regardless of where you start from, coming home is a feeling that can only be described as *delicious*. Enjoy the sweet-centeredness that comes from knowing you are what you needed all along and that you're about to unveil the truth within you.

CHAPTER 3

WHAT I MEAN BY FREQUENCY

Every morning, my partner Zack makes his special version of hot chocolate (what we call "Holy Cacao!"). This creamy drink is a rich, delectable way to start the day. Taking that first sip is truly heavenly, but even better is the time it gives us to enjoy together. As we sip, we talk about everything from our plans for the day to our dreams from the night before.

Sometimes, we even record our *Raw Spirituality* podcast over cups of Holy Cacao. The ritual of the drink serves as a way to anchor our connection to each other.

Want the recipe for our Holy Cacao? You can find it in the Resources section at the end of this book.

For you, maybe that type of anticipation comes from a perfectly ripe summer strawberry, a smear of freshly ground almond butter, or a glass of fine wine. Think about how much you enjoy your favorite treat—the taste, the texture, all the nourishment it offers to your body and soul. Hard to believe, isn't it, that for somebody out there, that same delicious treat could be downright dangerous?

For people who have food allergies or addictive tendencies, certain foods (even foods that most people think of as unequivocally healthy) can lead to serious sickness. The same chocolate drink I look forward to every morning could make someone with a cacao allergy break out in hives.

Would it surprise you to learn that the reverse is also true? I know folks who can eat a fast food burger and fries every day if they want to and experience no negative aftereffects whatsoever. I'm the opposite—my body reacts so strongly against any kind of processed food that I can't even eat organic (but processed) crackers without feeling a little sluggish afterward. I can only imagine what would happen if I indulged in fast food like some people do—I'm not going to experiment and find out!

This isn't only true about food. Maybe you know someone who has an allergy to medicine, such as sulfa drugs or penicillin. The same substance that saves lives all over the world will end their life if a well-meaning but uninformed doctor gives it to them.

The fact is that every aspect of your diet—again, in the broadest, most holistic sense of the word—has the potential to impact you in a vastly different way from how it impacts others.

That difference all depends on your frequency.

WHAT IS FREQUENCY?

Everything within our natural world, from humans to animals to inanimate elements, has a vibration, also known as its frequency. Each thing's overall frequency is, in turn, made up of the specific frequencies of the cells that compose it. As a human being, your individual frequency is the average of specific frequencies within your organs, which in turn have an average frequency composed from the frequency of the cells that they are made of.

Each thing's individual frequency is the code for their entire experience of being. As a human, your frequency is primarily based on your perception (your level of consciousness). Higher frequencies correspond to expansion and a given thing's natural state. When you engage in things that give you joy or put you in a state of contentment, your frequency rises. Meanwhile, lower frequencies result from constriction and moving farther away from your natural state. When you engage with sources of fear, anger, violence, or judgment, your frequency lowers.

Along with raising or lowering your frequency through the actions you take, you also absorb frequencies that come into your body through external sources. The food and drink you choose are a great example of how this works beyond the nutritional level. Anything you consume that is processed or dead will bring a lower frequency into your body. And when that lower frequency meets a higher frequency within your body, uncomfortable reactions are almost guaranteed. The higher your frequency, the faster the reaction (wanted or unwanted) in your physical and emotional bodies.

This is true of your food not only in its final form but also with respect to the frequencies it absorbed throughout its life. Each experience leaves that food with an energetic signature on its cells that contribute to its overall frequency.

For example, some might assume that dairy has an inherently higher frequency than meat, since it doesn't involve ingesting actual animal flesh. However, the dairy industry is in fact far more brutal than the meat industry, in terms of violence and slaughter. As a result, the frequency of dairy products tends to be just as low as meat, if not lower. The frequencies of terror, overwhelm, and pain don't cook out of animal products. When you consume them, you absorb the experiences those animals absorbed and incorporate their frequency into your own.

Depending on where your frequency happens to be at the time, this phenomenon may affect you powerfully, minimally, or not at all. If your frequency matches that pain energy, you may not notice its effect on you. But if your frequency is fairly high, or you generally feel great, eating something that contains that pain energy may cause you to feel tired, have trouble sleeping, or experience emotional issues like heightened anxiety or even obsessive-compulsive behavior. (Not surprising, since sometimes animals in that situation will exhibit OCD-like behaviors as a coping mechanism for the distress they feel.) In a mainstream, non-human-animal-eating diet, these symptoms have become so normalized that many people assume they are just part of their personal makeup.

Again, this isn't a matter of right and wrong. There's no reason to judge anyone, including yourself, for what you choose to consume. It's simply important to consider whether those choices help you reach the experience of life that you'd like to have. If you're ready to activate your intuition and elevate your spiritual consciousness, considering the frequency of what you consume is foundational to that goal.

OPENING UP TO THE NEW

As we said at the outset, the pineal gland helps you connect with your highest self, your intuitive sense, and your Divine Source energy. As your pineal gland vibrates at a higher frequency, you feel closer and more unified with your highest self and true nature.

But the process of raising your frequency isn't straightforward. As your frequency rises, the increased vibration begins to shake up your deepest held beliefs, even down to the conditioning layered in by other lifetimes, family upbringing, DNA imprinting, and the culture you were raised in. Like geological layers in an earthquake, those beliefs and distortions begin to dislodge, shift, and bubble up into the conscious mind. For perhaps the first time, you can bring those beliefs to light, understand where they came from, and feel whether they align with your true nature. This is where the waking up feeling comes from.

The waking up sensation isn't just a feeling. Science shows us that during the awakening process, crystals in the pineal gland respond to frequency with a charge that interacts with the electromagnetic field generated by the brain and heart. When those crystals are charged up from a high-frequency emotion like love or joy, they begin to vibrate really fast. This vibration expands your field to the point where it shakes off calcification that has accumulated in your pineal gland.

Again, the work of Dr. Joe Dispenza is very helpful for understanding what happens biospiritually as we raise consciousness. His book *Becoming Supernatural* goes deep into the science behind these crystals and their vibration.

That awakening puts you more in control of your beliefs. Instead of letting them provoke you to perceive the external world in predetermined ways, you can decide for yourself how to perceive. Instead of letting circumstances dictate whether you have a bad day, you grow more proactive with your energy. The beliefs that don't align fall away, and you find yourself open to new beliefs and ways of thinking.

When my cousin had cancer, she was in tremendous pain, and no medication seemed to help her. My family could see that she was nearing the moment of passing. Many of them felt overwhelming grief about the prospect of her death and felt increasing fear with each day that passed. But I, meanwhile, wasn't conscious of any sadness or fear. Instead, I was flooded with love for my cousin, gratitude for having had her in my life, and relief that she would no longer be in pain. Living at a high frequency allowed me to process her passing by tuning into the love I had for my family. I was flooded with so much love that I was able to be strong and supportive for them as they grieved her passing. We all cried together, but while some of my tears came from the deep empathy I feel for the loss of a loved one, the overwhelming love I felt for my family and my gratitude for the close bond we share was at the forefront of my heart.

From an outsider's perspective, it might have appeared that I didn't care enough about my cousin because I wasn't devastated by her death. But I wasn't worried with how others perceived me. After all, there isn't a right or wrong response to death. I'd simply trained myself to feel fully aligned with the overall experience of life that I want to have. Even as I acknowledged the loss of someone important to me, and allow myself to grieve and feel the loss, the dominant frequency I felt was love.

THE BIG PICTURE

As humans, we often ask ourselves why we are here and what our purpose is in life. Societal conditioning answers this question out of a low-frequency perspective. We may believe that the world isn't safe, that we live in a constant state of lack, that we have to work hard in order to survive, gain approval, and achieve what we want.

When you live in this low-frequency conditioning, your purpose in life becomes grasping for more. More love, more money, more attention, anything that caters to primal insatiable energy. No matter how good your situation might become, your egoic self will see it as not enough because you're seeing the world through a lens of desperation and lack.

But as your frequency rises, your clarity in purpose begins to emerge. Instead of feeling driven to grasp more for yourself, you become occupied with giving more to others. Your higher self knows that when you're in service—whether it be to other humans, to animals, or to the planet—you are also being taken care of. The higher your frequency rises, the more you believe that your needs will always be met, and the more you act in alignment with your true, authentic nature. This is not the same as having no boundaries or being a doormat. It's truly loving and caring for others while incorporating the wisdom of self-care.

This is, as you might imagine, a wonderful way to experience life. But it doesn't stop with just your perception. By simply living and acting from your heart center, you help those around you tune into their authentic nature and raise their frequency as well. Add to that, you also will begin to magnetize others who are heart focused and ready to awaken to their next level of love.

THE UNIFIED FIELD

As beings on this earth, we live within an electromagnetic field. This field of consciousness includes the universe and everything in it. To put it another way, we're all swimming in a soup made of ingredients that each of us has contributed to the pot.

Quantum physics refers to this as the "unified field." The unified field, among other things, carries information—information from the world outside that comes into each person that we respond to, as well as the information within each person that goes out into the world. Everything I project from my heart, feelings, and mind goes out through my brainwaves and heart waves into the unified field around me. The same is true of you, as well as animals, plants, rocks, and every living being on this planet. All of us, asleep or awake, are contributing to the unified field twenty-four hours a day.

In the late 1960s and early 1970s, a number of studies were carried out around collective consciousness. Monkeys were placed onto different islands. When a group of monkeys on

Despite being well studied, the unified field is widely misunderstood. But most of us have tuned into it at some point, intentionally or not. You probably can tell instantly when you walk into a room where two people have just had a fight. Even if there are no clues in their voices or expressions, you can feel the air crackling with tension and unspoken emotion.

The thought forms in the field have left an impression that you can intuitively notice.

If you're interested in learning about more unified field experiments, I recommend the book *Source Field Experiments* by David Wilcock.

Here's the really amazing thing: when you're operating from a higher frequency, you can actually help raise frequency where others have lowered it. Not only can you take responsibility for what you're contributing with your own emotions and thoughts, but you can also take action on behalf of others. You can be a steward of the environment by cleansing the unified field around you.

Many traditional cultures around the world have longstanding practices of cleansing the unified field. From ancient Egyptians to Native Americans, burning salvia or sage (known as smudging) has been passed down generation to generation to create an uplifted spiritual energy in their space. We know now that this practice not only clears low-vibe thought forms and energies but also bacteria and viruses lingering in the air. This is one of many examples of ancient practices being supported by today's science.

Consciously contributing to the unified field is much easier than it might seem. You don't have to constantly be performing heroic acts of service in order to transmit high-vibe energy into the field. That type of contribution certainly has value, but it's much simpler to contribute unconsciously through your perception of the world around you. Science tells us that the electrons that make up matter change their behavior based on the presence and resonance of whatever is observing them. To put it more simply, what you see changes in response to how you see it.

That's why it's backward to let your perception of the external world determine how you feel, but that's what most people are conditioned to do. If something happens that they don't like, they feel bad. When something "good" happens, then they feel good. In either case, they wonder why life keeps repeating the same type of situations and circumstances. When in reality, it's a case of a stimulus provoking a habituated perception and corresponding response that in themselves perpetuate the same type of situations over and over.

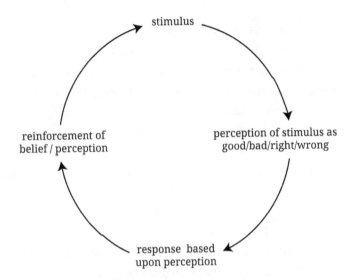

The truly natural state for humans is to first feel a certain way, then perceive the external world through the lens of that state of being. Living within your natural high-frequency blueprint allows you to contribute to the unified field by perceiving it with love, gratitude, and positivity, and receiving those vibrations back.

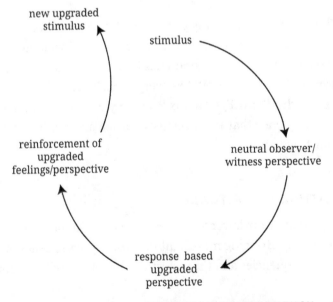

Over the years, I've had the opportunity to participate in professional trainings with the HeartMath Institute, a nonprofit research organization that studies how emotional and mental stress management influences your overall resilience and well-being. They carried out a series of experiments in which they hooked participants up to monitors that measured their electromagnetic field via heart rate variability. Participants were then shown randomized images that ranged from happy scenes of smiling faces to scenes of upsetting violence.

Researchers found that the participant's field registered a prestimulus response seconds before the computer had even selected the random image to display.

"Since emotional processes can work faster than the mind, it takes a power stronger than the mind to bend perception, override emotional circuitry, and provide us with intuitive feeling instead. It takes the power of the heart."

—DOC CHILDRE, HEARTMATH INSTITUTE FOUNDER

This shows that not only can you pick up quickly on signs and signals, but you can learn the language of your electromagnetic field, too. The brain has limits to how much it can process, but the field catches everything. That's why a large part of the Third Eye Diet is keeping your individual field in a frequency that is consciously chosen and aligned with your true nature.

SCIENCE + SPIRITUALITY

As you shift from lower to higher frequency, your body begins to detoxify. Bringing more light into your system pushes out lower frequencies and the distortion they create within your body's energy. Even though this change is for the better, it doesn't always make you feel amazing right away. Detoxifying distortion can impact you physically, emotionally, and mentally.

PHYSICAL

As you detoxify low frequencies, your physical body begins to purge and rebalance. Old health issues may resurface—for example, a person raising their frequency at age fifty might experience pain from a knee injury they sustained at age twenty. You might find yourself feeling sluggish as your filtration organs (primarily kidneys and liver) work overtime to cleanse your body of low-frequency pathogens.

EMOTIONAL

Spiritual awakening and emotional healing are closely intertwined, and it's common to have emotional releases as you clear low-frequency patterns. Sometimes, this can show up as crying or feeling anxiety or grief without even knowing why, or laughing uncontrollably as you release the tension that was trapped in the emotional body.

MENTAL

Some people experience mental fog or a feeling of detachment as they detoxify low frequencies. You might arrive at a destination and not remember how you got there, walk into a room and forget the reason you walked in, or you may feel as though your entire day is moving through a dream. Meanwhile, your actual dreams during sleep may start to feel incredibly real, offering you a look into multilayered expressions of your soul's experience.

One of my colleagues was recently working on clearing a number of beliefs she'd inherited through family conditioning. As she spoke about her parents, she started to get a cough. (Throat chakra issues like coughing are very common when you're detoxifying issues that have to do with expression.) Together, we worked on raising her frequency and healing distorted beliefs that she didn't feel that she had the right to speak her truth. As her body released the frequency created by her old patterns, the cough cleared. With the restoration of her physical health came a renewed ability to express herself freely, clearly, and truthfully.

Be assured that initial discomfort is definitely worth the release of conditioned behaviors, beliefs, and ways of thinking that have reinforced fear and anxiety throughout your life. As you progress, you'll release your primary investment in the material world. This means that the more your frequency rises, the more you'll recognize the material world as a way to support your human experience, not as the be-all-end-all of your experience.

PROVIDE A SUPPORTIVE ENVIRONMENT FOR YOUR WHOLE SELF

In the process of raising your frequency, the most important thing you can do is provide a supportive environment for yourself. Just as you keep a cut clean to help it heal, you want to create an environment in which your body, mind, and spirit are able to release old conditioning and rebuild in alignment with your new higher frequency.

To support yourself in this process, it can be helpful to know exactly what's going on in your body. From a scientific perspective, we know that each cell within the body contains a microtubule that vibrates at a certain wavelength. This is the frequency we can actually measure in the physical world. Each part of the body—bones, organs, fluids, etc.—vibrates at the average frequency of the cells that make it up.

Depending on what your personal conditioning consists of, different parts of your body are likely vibrating at different frequencies. For example, your kidneys could have a frequency of 420 hz while your thymus is vibrating at 200 hz. Your overall frequency is the average of all these different frequencies in each individual organ and cell. But the overall frequency affects each individual organ as well. Raising your body's overall frequency creates holistic energetic harmony that can be felt throughout your body, and even within the metaphysical aspects of your being, where the vibration is too high to be measured.

HOW FREQUENCY IS CREATED

This brings up an important point about how frequency is created in the first place. As much as we might try to consciously correct our response to stress, our bodies, minds, and spirits respond according to the conditioning we received.

I described earlier how my childhood was characterized by a huge amount of anxiety. I was able to perceive multidimensionally—seeing people who had passed on, witnessing different times and places, past and future. But because I was immersed in a religious environment that conditioned me to understand the paranormal as bad and frightening, those experiences became a source of stress in my life instead of inspiring a sense of curiosity or wonder.

No matter how hard we try to avoid encountering stressful or unhealthy situations, life will often offer them to us to learn through. This is especially true about childhood, when most people don't have enough knowledge or personal agency to get out of an unhealthy situation. But it's important to remember that stress or situations don't cause problems—our response does.

As a child, I responded to stress by learning to never fully relax. "Normal" for me meant holding a constant low-level anxiety, especially at night. I ran at breakneck speed through dark hallways, hoping to avoid what I might see there and regularly struggled to fall asleep. And because I didn't feel like I could talk about what was happening to me (not only did I not have the words, but I felt like nobody had the answers), my throat chakra became tightly constricted, causing unseen harm to my thyroid. Meanwhile, the self-judgment that lodged in my high heart chakra affected my thymus gland, which is the seat of the immune system.

With my immune system working overtime to heal the growing dysfunction in my organs, all my genetic switches were thrown. That was how I eventually came to be diagnosed with Graves' disease, a syndrome that is commonly understood as the immune system attacking the thyroid gland. By the time I was a teenager, 99.9 percent of my thyroid gland had been surgically removed.

In retrospect, it all makes perfect sense. The incredibly high frequency of my third eye and crown chakras, which enabled me to see and hear multidimensional things, were in conflict with the constriction of my throat and high heart caused by lack of expression, fear, and self-judgment. While the high frequencies in my body gave me a glowing appearance of love so bright that others would comment on it, my repressed constriction and fear were causing my physical health to break down. Energetically speaking, all autoimmune disease/disorder is based on a recurring underlying inner conflict.

For a long time, I assumed everyone had the same paranormal perception as me and were somehow coping with it better than I did. I felt, as children often do, that something must be uniquely wrong with me. Later, though, I realized that everyone around me *wasn't* having the same experiences. Instead of making me feel better, this realization made me feel even more isolated. I was desperate to experience life like my sister did. She didn't have trouble going to sleep at night. She wasn't running down the hall because an unseen entity was pulling her hair.

Interestingly, my sister and I have both had our DNA tested and discovered that we both have the gene for Graves' disease. However, my sister's gene has never been switched on because her individual frequencies have not been in conflict in the way mine were. (She, by the way, is one of those people described in the beginning of this chapter, who can eat pretty much whatever she wants and not have any apparent consequences.)

You may already know that genes often get switched on by trauma. In my case, the trauma came from the death of my grandmother, the first death I'd ever experienced in this lifetime. I was too young to recognize or articulate the way her death affected me, especially because I didn't see my experience reflected in others. My sister was also close with my grandmother, but she didn't experience trauma in the same way that I did, probably for the same reason that certain foods don't impact us in the same way. Neither experience was right or wrong, better or worse. It's just a matter of how each person's individual frequency is affected.

This illustrates how important it is not to write off your own experiences just because others haven't experienced them the same way. Trauma comparison or not dealing with a trauma doesn't stop it from dealing with you, regardless if others didn't even translate the same experience as trauma at all. Self-honoring is a skill that you can expect to naturally grow alongside your spiritual activation.

As I grew older and learned about raising my frequency, I began to accept and even welcome my paranormal perception. As that conditioning of fear and self-judgment fell away, I found a new ability to speak from my heart. This raised the frequency of my throat and high heart, causing my health to improve by leaps and bounds. Before long, I sensed a conscious desire growing within me that some would call crazy: I wanted to grow my thyroid back.

My doctor assured me that this was impossible. Some organs can regenerate, he told me, but the thyroid isn't one of them. But the more I lived in my state of high frequency, the more I felt convinced that my thyroid gland was in fact growing back. Finally, I went to the doctor and requested an ultrasound. To my doctor's astonishment, the ultrasound showed one-fourth of a regenerated thyroid on one side, one-third on the other.

Understandably, my doctor was freaked out. He'd never seen anything like what was happening in my body. But to me, it made perfect sense. When you remove the low-frequency conditions, the body is free to heal, expand, and recover its natural state. I'm still in the process of allowing my body to move into its next level of regeneration. I'll keep you posted!

WAKE UP THE REBEL WITHIN YOU

When you begin the process of raising frequency, it may feel like an uphill climb. Parts of the detoxification process are challenging, especially when they bring up issues or memories that you thought you'd already fully recovered from.

The physical body is like a recorder; it saves *every* experience, thought, and feeling that moves through your electromagnetic field. Even if you don't have a conscious memory of something, it still lives within you, and can provoke reactions to stimuli related to that experience. This has been confirmed through kinesiology, muscle testing, and modalities such as hypnosis.

The base-level source of your frequency, however, is your soul's curriculum. Before you incarnated in physical form, your soul chose a certain set of experiences for this lifetime— not to hurt you but to help you.

This can cause confusion and pain if it's not understood clearly. For example, one of my clients was raised by alcoholic parents, which has created challenges for her throughout her entire life. For a long time, she blamed them for creating chaos in her world. But as she has activated her third eye, she has learned to see that situation from a higher level of consciousness. Today, she sees what can be *gained* from growing up in such a difficult, painful situation. Her experience has given her a unique perspective on love, childhood, and parenting, one that is vital and healing for her to share with the world. This perception doesn't negate her pain; it just allows for the underlying purpose of the experience to begin to shine through, healing the wounds along the way.

The same thing is true for me. I truly believe that the way I'm serving people today is partly a result of my childhood experiences. Experiencing my own life-threatening physical issues, and the chronic childhood fear that provoked them, created a level of empathy for others that allows me to be extremely effective in my work. Now that I know how to hold my own energy, I'm not scared of it anymore, and there's nothing that a client can bring up that rattles my field.

That's why when you're in this process, it's incredibly helpful to focus on gratitude. It's an amazing gift that as humans, we are designed to manipulate our own frequencies and hold our own energy. You don't have to sit and wait for higher consciousness to descend upon you. You're hardwired to access it by shifting your own frequency.

This should give so much hope to anyone who has felt like they're a victim of intensely constrictive circumstances or conditioning. There's no denying that when circumstances like this take place in your life, they become deeply embedded within you, sometimes even within your DNA. But as raising frequency brings your beliefs to the surface, you can make a conscious choice about whether or not you choose to continue to carry those beliefs within your energy field. Once your frequency rises to a critical point, you won't even have to make the choice anymore. Your system will simply discard lower, distorted frequencies naturally and instinctively.

This is further proof that moving from constriction to expansion is a normal evolutionary process. The only reason it might seem like a revolution is because our collective consciousness has normalized staying in one place. (More specifically, staying in a fear-based place.) Change is viewed as revolutionary when, in reality, higher consciousness is the norm. We are meant to live our lives from that perspective.

You aren't at the mercy of your past circumstances. Your life is within your control, and you have the power to choose the experiences you wish to have. While today it may seem like the journey is long, I want you to be encouraged by the process you've already set in place. An awakened soul cannot coexist with complacency. As you awaken the third eye and raise your frequency, you activate your natural sovereignty. Instead of your past defining you, it transmutes into wisdom. This allows for the openness required to choose present states of being that will create a future aligned with what you truly desire. It's an exciting process of rebellion.

Two things can help in this process:

1. Be conscious of your reactions. Every response you have to your circumstances today is setting the stage for what you'll experience tomorrow. Practice becoming the neutral observer, the compassionate witness to your feelings. Affirming, "I am not my feelings; I am the neutral observer," can be super helpful during this phase.
2. Keep in mind that you might be the only person in your family or friendship circle who is starting to make conscious choices. Allow them to have their responses without judgment from you and then choose whether or not you'll allow their responses to deter you from your

path. Soon enough, you'll start to magnetize other people who are doing the same thing by not following what their environment taught them to believe.

THE ESSENCE

Right now, there are two camps on the planet: those who are sleepwalking, their spiritual eyes closed, and those who are awakening, opening their eyes and making conscious choices.

My hope is that this book will support you in becoming an alchemist. You'll learn how to shift frequencies, starting out by practicing and then, over time, moving into mastery. This includes every aspect of your environment—what you eat, drink, and watch.

In Chapter 6, you'll learn how to get specific about what you're offering into the quantum field and how to orchestrate a unification between the mind, body, and spirit.

As the third eye awakens and you raise frequency, you enter into the expansion process. In doing so, you start to leave behind distortion, and you begin to retrain the physical aspect of your body. In essence, you're going back to a state which you may or may not actually remember from this lifetime, but your soul and spirit do. As you activate the lightbody, you offer a specific contribution into the unified field while manifesting exactly what you want to receive back.

CHAPTER 4

COHERENCE

It created a bit of a stir in my hometown church when I walked in with a mohawk haircut. It was the eighties, and as a teenager devoted to the decade's edgy music scene, the haircut felt like a way to assert my personal identity. I expected a judgmental reaction, and I got it—lots of double takes, some sideways looks, and plenty of whispering.

But the one person I didn't fear any judgmental reaction from was Brother Bob. He was the pastor of this Southern Baptist congregation, and he was the least judgmental person I'd ever met in my life. Every Sunday, he would stand at the front of the church as soon as it opened, greeting everyone who came through the door with a loving gratitude for their presence. When church was over, he stood in the same place, shaking hands, giving hugs, thanking each person for attending.

There was something so special about how Brother Bob interacted with people. When he said your name, smiled, or even just made eye contact, you felt an overwhelming sense of acceptance. He made you feel like you were a source of blessing in his life, just by being there. And I believe that's genuinely how he felt. Even the sight of me with my edgy hair didn't change his reaction—he looked at me with the same loving acceptance, the same open heart that saw me as a blessing. I didn't feel like he even noticed my hair, and if he did, it wasn't lowering his opinion of me.

At the time, of course, I didn't know what I was observing in him. I just felt that he had something very special inside him, something that made me feel special, too. As an adult, I now can identify that as the feeling of being in a highly coherent state.

INTUITION + INCOHERENCE

As we mentioned in the introduction, being intuitive isn't a gift that some have and some don't. Everyone is naturally intuitive and has spiritual gifts available to them—it's just a matter of knowing how to access those gifts. When someone says, "I'm not an intuitive person," what they're really saying is that they're not in a coherent state.

Incoherence is what stands between people in the modern world and access to their intuition. Being in an incoherent state means that the signals from the two branches of your autonomic nervous system (ANS) are out of sync. This leads to low heart rate variability (HRV), usually without any noticeable physical symptoms. This low HRV results in the neural signals sent from the heart to the brain actually inhibiting higher cognitive functions, including intuition. Simply stated, incoherence prevents you from connecting with your highest self.

Here are a few clues as to what incoherence feels like:

- A low-level, ongoing resentment. You find your thoughts returning again and again to someone or something that bothers you—your current circumstances, your upbringing or events in your past, world events or actions from the government, etc. This includes an inability to forgive yourself or others.
- Superficial happiness without deep, abiding joy. You may think of yourself as a happy person, but you're easily tossed about by circumstances and find it hard to stay in a balanced, joyful state.
- A sense of burnout. You feel like you just don't have the energy to deal with life, or perhaps you find yourself withdrawing from people and activities for no apparent reason.
- A low-level feeling of overwhelm that either comes and goes, or comes and stays. Even just returning a phone call might seem like too much to deal with.
- A consistent state of worry. You might not identify as being anxious, but you experience an ongoing state of worry about life—what will happen in the future, how people think about you when you walk into a room, whether you're running late, how you'll get everything done you need to do.
- Mental fog, memory issues, or an inability to concentrate or focus. You might have a hard time making decisions. When you're called upon to determine what the best option is, you may get flustered, overwhelmed, or frozen with confusion. Frustration or impatience becomes a common state in daily life.
- Stagnating physical performance. You feel more drained by physical exertion, less coordinated in how you move, or your physical recovery takes longer.
- You feel confused or unclear on what your heart really wants. Even if you believe in guides or spirits, you feel as

though you can't hear what they're telling you. You feel distance in your connection with loved ones who have passed.

Strange as it may sound, being in an incoherent state can be addictive for many people. Even though being in a constant state of (even low-level) stress, worry, and resentment doesn't sound like a great way to live, there are certain payoffs that come with it.

The first one is familiarity. Living in a state of incoherence is common among the vast majority of people in today's world. From one day to the next, most people spend their lives just responding to external events. They get up for work, fight traffic on their way, and cope with stress, anxiety, and confusion as they focus mainly on the problems in their life and look for solutions. Even if they have a good attitude about those problems, it doesn't take them out of an incoherent state. They're so used to living this way that it feels normal, and normal feels safe. In fact, giving up this state of worry feels downright irresponsible to them, i.e., "If you're not worried, you're not paying attention."

Another so-called advantage to being in an incoherent state is that it's culturally and societally acceptable. When the majority of other people around you are off balance, worried, overwhelmed, and caught up in a response to external events, the idea of shifting into a different state can feel frightening.

This was certainly the case for me. Growing up, I never felt like I belonged anywhere, but staying incoherent let me feel, for once, like part of the tribe. I could share in the stressed response to external events that is so commonplace in our world.

Living in an incoherent state is like driving with one foot on the gas pedal and the other foot on the brake. As you alternate—gas, brake, gas, brake—you move forward, but only slightly, and with a lot of turbulence and discomfort. From a spiritual standpoint, when you live in incoherence, your mood and perspective on life jerk back and forth depending on the external circumstances you experience. Someone gives you great news, and you're filled with hope and confidence; the next day, or even the next minute, something terrible happens, and you're back in the depths of worry and resentment. In your up moments, you're able to open yourself to inspiration and pursue your spiritual calling, but then a down moment comes along and sets you back several steps. Your path to higher spiritual consciousness is clear, but your ability to move is hampered by the burden of an incoherent state.

PERCEPTION + COHERENCE

There once was a wise old farmer whose horse ran away.

When his neighbor heard about this, he said, "That's so unfortunate."

"It's hard to tell," the wise old farmer replied.

Three days later, the horse came trotting back into town with a wild horse following him.

"Instead of one horse, now you have two. That's wonderful!" the neighbor said.

"It's hard to tell," the wise old farmer said again.

The next day, while the farmer's son was trying to train the new wild horse, he fell and broke his leg.

When the neighbor heard about the broken leg, he said, "Your strong, healthy son is now a cripple—that's so unfortunate."

Again, the wise old farmer replied, "It's hard to tell."

A week later, the military came to take all the able-bodied young men to war. But because of the farmer's son's injury, he was left to stay with his family.

Hearing about the son being spared, the neighbor said to the farmer, "Your son might be injured, but at least he won't have to risk his life fighting in the war. That's so fortunate."

By now, you know what the wise old farmer had to say.

This parable illustrates something about the way life works when you're in a coherent state. Living in a constant state of reaction means always bouncing up and down depending on the circumstances. It's a fraught, turbulent way to live, and it can be very taxing on your body, mind, and spirit.

But when you live in a coherent state, like the wise old farmer, your experience of life is overlit with a transcendent, encompassing peace. You live in the confidence that *all is well*, even if you can't predict what's going to happen. At the same time, you experience a calm, positive alertness that puts you in flow with any situation you encounter. You trust the process of life, which empowers you to do your part in each situation. You can honor your responsibilities and make decisions, while also managing your emotions, your mental state, and your overall well-being.

Coherence creates this stable feeling through a number of scientifically proven factors. First and foremost, being in a coherent state creates a high level of HRV and puts your nervous system into sync. Everything is enhanced, from your mental and physical functioning to your emotional intelligence and spiritual connection. You become better at adapting to new situations, responding to challenges, and thriving in unfamiliar environments.

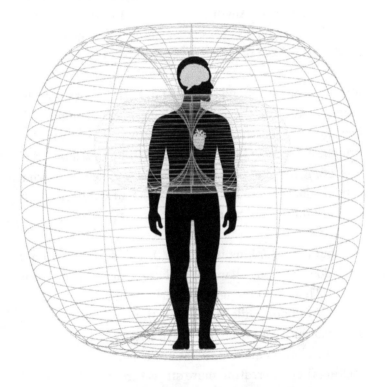

The physiological and psychological benefits of coherence have actually influenced some Olympic athletes to use coherence training to push their physical performance off the charts.

Then there's the impact of coherence on your intuition. This often starts with noticing quicker reaction times in moments of high need. Imagine someone rushes into your house with an emergency and you need to make a quick decision. In an incoherent state, you'll likely become flustered or freeze. But in a coherent state, you're able to start taking action without really thinking about it.

This exact thing happened to me several years ago. My father was visiting me in Austin, and one day I noticed a look of pain and panic on his face. When I asked him if he was okay, he shook his head no.

My father has sustained a number of heart attacks over the years, and that was the first thing that came to my mind. If I'd been in an incoherent state, I probably would have panicked. I might have wasted time trying to get him to tell me what was wrong or calling my mother or sister to figure out what I should do. But because I was in a coherent state, I instantly dropped into the moment.

Without even thinking it through, I took decisive action. I knelt down and put a hand on his knee so he would feel comforted. Then, even though my heart was pounding, I dialed 911 on my phone while at the same time pulling his license and insurance card from his wallet. Being in a highly coherent state allowed me to do what needed to be done without wasting time or creating more stress through a fear-based response to the situation. It was almost like being in a creative flow. I didn't have to think; instead, something took over that allowed me to choose the right actions in the right moment.

The really amazing thing is that at that time, coherence was not a constant habit for me. I was still building my baseline, practicing getting into a state of coherence every day. It shows how powerful coherence is that even a foundational level can accurately guide our emotions, thoughts, and actions in a moment of real crisis.

HOW COHERENCE SHIFTS RESPONSE

So how exactly does coherence transform the incoherent responses we're accustomed to? Every incoherent emotional response is related to a coherent emotion—the difference is that the response is lower on the frequency scale. Moving into a coherent state pushes that low-frequency worry into a high-frequency response of excitement and courage. Low-frequency stress becomes high-frequency passion. Boredom and complacency become contentment and fulfillment.

In the past, whenever I was about to teach a class or be interviewed for the radio, a podcast, or TV, I had a tendency toward feeling anxious. I wanted to do a good job, and I recognized that there might be people in the audience who didn't share my beliefs, and a part of me was anticipating being judged. But I realized that I always have a choice: either I can feel anxious about their different opinions and worry that they'll judge my ability to communicate or who they think I am, or I can feel excited to share my message and hear their points of view.

I started a practice of reminding myself that anxiety is one step away from excitement. This thought moves me into a coherent state, where I'm no longer concerned with defending myself or catering to my ego by trying to make sure everyone thinks the same way I do.

Instead, I feel excited about my mission and responsibility to share love and feel ready to keep my heart open for anyone sharing theirs.

When you move into a coherent state, you no longer get that consistent validation of being part of the tribe (if your tribe, like most, lives in an incoherent state). However, you feel so good in this coherent state you don't care. You're no longer driven by external validation. Instead, you're supported from within, which then shifts your current tribe or attracts a new one.

This reveals yet another wonderful benefit of coherence. By shifting low-frequency emotions into high-frequency emotions, it improves your ability to tap into your own potential. Without constantly worrying or looking out for threats, you're free and empowered to do what you showed up to do. Needless to say, this transforms your experience of life on the planet. When you release fear, threat, and defensiveness, you can step openly into any situation with love, excitement, and power.

On a metaphysical level, this process is moving your dominant energy from the lower, survival-centered chakras up into the heart, which is a gateway to the centers of inspiration, connection, and expression. Instead of having your actions based within your own insecurity, safety, and sense of duality (inferiority/superiority, good/bad, right/wrong), your heart is leading your experience.

This brings us back to the central modality for higher spiritual consciousness. Remember, we're not seeking some unattainable superpower. Rather, we're moving toward the most natural state of being for all living things, which just happens to be a supernatural (as in a really, *really* natural) power. Since constriction is a hallmark of an incoherent state, it stands to reason that by moving into a coherent state, you trigger expansion. As you expand, just like that, your levels of consciousness and frequency start to rise with no struggle or effort required.

FREQUENCY + COHERENCE

By now, you might be wondering how coherence is any different from frequency. While they play a similar role in the journey to higher spiritual consciousness, they aren't the same thing. You can have a high frequency while still being in and out of coherence.

However, raising your frequency opens the door to coherence, and being in a state of coherence automatically raises frequency. The two work together like cogs on adjoining wheels, opening the door to higher levels of consciousness.

In the latter half of the twentieth century, psychiatrist David R. Hawkins began to see common levels of thinking, feeling, and acting among the thousands of patients he had treated. He realized that people's challenges and advances depend on their level of consciousness. He first outlined a scale measuring levels of consciousness or vibration, named the Hawkins Map of Consciousness, in his *New York Times* bestselling book *Power Versus Force* (1995).

Over a period of more than twenty-five years, Dr. Hawkins, along with a group of researchers, used kinesiology to measure the level of consciousness in everything they could imagine:

people, books, music, events, countries, locations. Dr. Hawkins documented these consciousness levels on a scale from 1 to 1,000. On this scale, 200 is the level above which we begin to add energy to everything around us. Below 200, we are net consumers of energy. A few of these levels are:

- Shame, vibrating at 20.
- Fear at 100.
- Courage at 200.
- Acceptance at 350.
- Love at 500.
- Enlightenment levels range from 600 to 1000.

Today, tens of thousands of students and practitioners in multiple disciplines use the Hawkins Map to measure and affect change in quality of life and personal evolution. His work proves that everything has consciousness, that it can be measured, and that it can change.

Focused Life Force Energy, or FLFE (the service that creates a positive energetic environment that supports the consciousness of your space and gives you more energy to improve the quality of your life), is based on the Hawkins Level of Consciousness map. You'll notice easier, deeper meditation, overall uplifting feelings, support for physical and emotional healing, and a whole lot more. We are never without our Fluffy (FLFE)! Because it made such an extraordinary difference in our lives, I've partnered with them! You can get a fifteen-day free trial—just go to FLFE.net/alyssa or use the QR code here. We've also included links to some of the company's 5G studies and other research in the Resources section at the end of this book.

In general, frequency is the most subject to variation based on response to situations. This variation directly relates to your level of consciousness. People often have high frequency in one specific area of their life—for example, when talking about their grandchildren or when engaged in a job that they love—even while having a low overall frequency. That indicates that these people might not have a high level of spiritual consciousness or a coherent state as their baseline.

Coherence is far less susceptible to situation-based variations. It's more a way of life. As you practice it, it becomes a physical, emotional, mental, and spiritual pattern anchored within your nervous system.

Let's say you feel an overall lack of excitement about your circumstances. You notice that this feeling isn't aligning with how you want to experience life. You'd like to feel super excited about your life and be grateful and inspired, no matter what comes your way.

Most people assume that the only way to create this shift is to trade their life in for a brand-new one—move to a new city, break up with their current partner and find a new one, ditch their job and start working in a different industry, etc. However, when you're awakening and activating spiritually, you start to feel the importance of working *with* the unified field instead of against it. You change your perspective and emotional state first and then watch how the external situations shift in response.

It's true; this awareness indicates a higher level of spiritual consciousness than we might consider average at this time. You might even feel that the only way to have that new perspective and emotional state is through a divine act of grace, i.e., a miracle. When you're pulled up and down the frequency spectrum by everything that happens to you and around you, how are you supposed to intentionally move into a higher level of consciousness?

The answer is through practicing coherence. This state brings a beautiful blend of invincibility and vulnerability. You know that you don't have all the answers to all of life's questions, but you feel centered in what you've learned while still being open to new ideas. Your life view becomes more hopeful and harmonious. In the words of Dr. David R. Hawkins, "This way of life is meaningful, complete, perfect and serene."

However, the best way to understand what coherence feels like is to get there yourself. So why don't we take a moment for you to try on a coherent state and find out for yourself?

HOW TO GET INTO A COHERENT STATE

There are several different techniques to get into a state of coherence, but I'm sharing my favorite one. It's based on research from the HeartMath Institute, slightly adjusted for our purposes here.

Before you get started, choose a renewing or rejuvenating emotion that you can draw from during the exercise, such as appreciation and compassion. A great place to start is with a memory. You could reflect on thoughts of a beloved family member (or even a pet) who is healthy and well. You could call to mind the most wonderful, relaxing beach trip you ever had. You could think back to a special moment with your partner or a wonderful success you experienced in the past.

If you don't have a specific memory, you can focus on bringing up a sense of appreciation and gratitude for something in the present moment. For example, every morning when I wake up, I appreciate that I have a soft pillow, a clean place to sleep, hot water for my shower, and clean water to drink. Just by focusing on these simple sources of gratitude, I instantly activate a coherent state.

For some people, the exercise of gratitude can be burdened by the thought of how many people in the world don't have the same blessings. It may feel selfish and elitist to simply reflect on the good things you have. You may experience a sense of guilt for spending this time on your own state, instead of doing something to help others.

While it's natural to have compassion and a heart to support others, resisting gratitude is still symptomatic of a neural pathway trained for incoherence. Anxiety and resentment don't stop being low-frequency emotions just because you're feeling them on behalf of others. Should a doctor get sick to show empathy and support to his patients?

Fortunately, you can easily turn these feelings into a renewing, coherent emotion without losing your sense of compassion and motivation. After focusing on your gratitude for what you have, add in a sense of gratitude that you're in a position to take action on behalf of all the people who don't have the same support that you do. Follow it up with taking real action—as soon as your coherence practice is done, notice what you're inspired to do. You may be moved to hop on your computer and make a donation to provide clean water for a struggling community, or you may feel that some time spent in prayer for the well-being of all of the earth's children is what your heart is directing.

Moving into a coherent state is never irresponsible or elitist. Focusing your awareness on these positive emotions is essential prework for the process of changing the world.

COHERENCE EXERCISE

Focus on the area behind the sternum in the center of your chest. Imagine or intend that you're breathing directly in and out of the heart center. As you breathe in and out of your heart center, slow down your breath. Try inhaling for five seconds and exhaling for five seconds. Find the rhythm that works for you.

In your mind, as you breathe in, say the word that describes your current feeling around that treasured memory, or even just the word for desired emotional state: compassion, gratitude, or peace, for example. Imagine breathing that word into your chest. On the exhale, let the energy of that word fill your entire body and expand into the field around you. When you breathe in again, breathe in that word.

While you breathe, make a sincere attempt to experience the regenerative feeling of your chosen word. Breathe in and out of the heart center and allow yourself to expand that feeling.

Throughout this process, many people feel sensations of warmth or tingling in their chest as it responds to your consciousness. That's a good sign—it's the sensation of expansion. Your mind will most likely wander, but that's nothing to worry about—it doesn't decrease the effect of the exercise. Just focus on your breath while also holding the uplifting emotion for as long as you can. And don't worry if you don't feel anything, it takes time and practice, and some of us are more kinesthetic than others.

Continue the process for as long as you can sustain it. If your mind wanders, just redirect to the area in the center of the chest, and the energy of the word you've chosen.

You can find this exercise, along with a related coherence exercise from the HeartMath Institute, in the Resources section at the back of this book.

COHERENCE IN REAL TIME

No matter what you're grateful for, this exercise will help move you into a coherent state.

You'll find that the more you practice, the easier it gets and the more natural it feels.

I do this exercise every morning when I wake up and again when I arrive at my office. Before I start contributing (the word I use for work), I focus on my heart center. As I breathe in and out of my chest, I look out the window and see the gorgeous trees that surround the building. In that moment, I feel so much gratitude for the shade and beauty the trees provide. The green colors are so rich. The birds have built homes there. I feel so appreciative that we share the planet with such amazing living beings like these. Then I intentionally feel deep gratitude for the opportunity, skill, and talent to do the work that I do, for how I get to teach and learn at the same time, and I top it off with immense appreciation for my clients and students. After this, I'm all set, super coherent, ready to contribute with no-holds-barred love.

As you incorporate this coherence technique into your daily routine, you'll become more aware of your mind. You'll notice what triggers you, what distracts you, and where your mind wanders. By gaining awareness, you're losing the lower frequency judgmental patterns you have received through conditioning. *You're in the process of training yourself to lose that low-vibe conditioning and consciously choose how you want to feel.*

As you practice, you may notice that memories or old physical issues start to surface at times. The emotions of gratitude and compassion have a higher light quotient than the emotions of worry and overwhelm, and a higher light quotient equals less density. By bringing in higher frequencies, you're lowering density and displacing worry, frustration, and sadness. It's an up-and-out healing phenomenon.

One of my clients has been working on coherence for four weeks. As I was guiding her in the coherence process, I encouraged her to sustain her state for about ten minutes. Before the ten minutes were up, she was crying. When I asked what the tears were about, she said she didn't know. Honoring and holding space for her experience, we let them flow. She continued to focus on the heart center and breathing compassion in and out of her chest. When we finished the exercise, the aha moment arrived. She realized that, having always been a perfectionist, she'd held herself to a ridiculously high standard (common for those of us who are old souls). After spending so many years not having compassion for herself, this new state was an enormous relief. By moving into coherence, she was able to relax and turn her compassion inward. Crying was her way of releasing that long-held tension and allowing relief to flood her body. The tears were a physical, emotional, mental, and spiritual detox.

Recently, I was speaking with a family member when I felt

a sudden, stabbing pain in my back. I breathed through it, and a few moments later, it went away. When I asked the pain what it was there to teach me, I realized I was holding the repressed energy of grief around a person that my family member was talking about. In that fleeting moment, the energy showed up as physical pain. But by continuing to listen to my family member while focusing on breathing love in and out of my heart center, I was able to resolve the pain and the repressed grief, all at once. Coherence provided the landscape and the mechanism for healing an old, unresolved wound that I wasn't even aware of.

Not only does practice make it easier to get into a coherent state, but it becomes easier to maintain it. Once you've changed your baseline, you'll find yourself naturally falling into a coherent state. Your overall baseline of coherence adjusts. Based on studies, developing a coherent state requires, on average, fifteen minutes of practice twice a day for six weeks. Obviously, some people will take longer, while others will shift more quickly. The bottom line is that if you keep at it consistently, you will change your baseline.

CHALLENGES TO COHERENCE

As you begin cultivating a coherent state, it can be helpful to be aware of the challenges you may encounter along the way.

EXTERNAL CHALLENGES

First, there is the challenge to your internal baseline. We've used this word a few times now—it refers to your automatic response to circumstances, ideas, or influences from others. That response is set by your amygdala, a part of the brain that functions as the emotional thermostat of the body. For example, you might roll your eyes, feel anger, bitterness, or some other form of stress anytime someone mentions your ex.

Coherence starts with rebuilding your baseline as a stable foundation in your nervous system. That physical baseline also supports you emotionally, mentally, and spiritually by reconditioning your automatic defaults and encouraging your amygdala to send out different signals. This process is known as *progressive repatterning*. Soon enough, your progress becomes totally automated. With that new baseline in place, you're able to move up those levels of consciousness.

Another type of challenge occurs within your relationships and community. While coherence is highly contagious, not everyone will be open to receive the energy of love or appreciation that you're generating. But that doesn't matter. What matters is that you're being responsible for what you radiate into the world. In the process, you're also creating a template for others to integrate into their own life, if they so choose.

Imagine a family of ten people, in which one of those people is forgiving and loving, while everyone else is worried, resentful, or bitter. Chances are that at least some people in the family will take advantage of that coherent template and start moving into that state themselves, even without realizing they're doing it. Others may be resistant to feeling better and resist shifting toward love, forgiveness, and gratitude. That's okay—it simply means they're not finished learning from incoherence.

The good news is that coherence is its own protection. Even if your coherent state means there are fewer physical people around you, you'll feel less isolated than before. That's because the nature of coherence is to create a feeling of unity. While incoherent people experience loneliness and isolation even in a big group (thanks to the superficial connections created by incoherent emotions), coherent people feel a deeper sense of connection with all living beings. No matter where you are or what you're doing, there's a sense that we're all in this together.

INTERNAL CHALLENGES

There's also the challenge that comes from within you. As much as incoherence creates blockage, it can also lead to emotions that have certain uses for different stages in your journey. For example, imagine someone who seems dead set on feeling angry—the smallest annoyances can cause them to verbally attack someone who they believe wronged them.

Chances are they are that way because their anger is teaching them something. Maybe they're feeling empowered for the first time because they're finally moving up the frequency ladder from depression to anger. Where they used to swallow their rage, now they feel powerful because they're able to express it and use it to change their situation. This person isn't ready to move into a coherent state because they don't want to lose that newfound powerful energy.

If you discover that you're not ready to move out of incoherence yet, it's okay. Every emotion is appropriate for a specific time, and every human knows within themselves what is right for them at a given time. For that reason, it's not accurate or useful to make sweeping generalizations like "peace is better than anger," or to say that certain emotions should always be avoided. They are what I call "slingshot energies," meaning they can be an effective way to move between states of being and can offer the boost you need for a time. A good example is when a depressed person begins to feel energized by feelings of anger. It's not peace and joy yet, but it's a stepping stone that lifts the heavy, inactive veil of depression and generates feelings of action and focus. The next step is courage, and it's now accessible because it's just a small step up the frequency/level-of-consciousness ladder.

Another internal challenge to coherence is unfamiliarity. We tend to unconsciously avoid change when we're still learning from a situation, even if we consciously really want to make that change. Internally, you may feel safer or more comfortable with the familiar than with growth or expansion. Sometimes, this is accompanied by a payoff, which encourages us to hold on to the old pattern. For example, if someone is ill, their family might call them all the time to check up on them. When they're healthy and doing great, nobody ever calls. Naturally, that person equates the familiarity of being ill with being safe and loved, so they unconsciously resist change.

All of that being said, *the soul's natural state is freedom.* When your soul is tired of feeling frustrated, confined, and constricted, you'll feel motivated to not only practice coherence yourself but also surround yourself with a community of coherence. Like attracts like, after all—the more you're in a coherent state yourself, the more you'll attract things and people in a coherent state, even if these aren't within your usual circle. You'll be drawn to books, films, conversations, groups of people, and even careers and places to live that can help you be in a coherent state.

There's a growing community of humans who are prioritizing coherent states. If you're interested in connecting with those people and seeing how coherence is changing the planet, check out the HeartMath Global Coherence Initiative (Heart-Math.org/gci/). You'll see a map that shows how many people are recording their coherence using a coherence monitor at any given time and become part of a global community of heart-based beings.

We've included this link in the Resources section at the end of this book, as well as a source for obtaining your own monitor for coherence training.

Along with this physical community, becoming coherent aligns you with your multidimensional community. All of your highest and purest guides, angels, and ascended masters are coherent. When you raise frequency and coherence and ascend your level of consciousness, you're shortening the perceived distance between your consciousness and the consciousness of higher beings. It's like picking up the phone and having someone on the other end of the line before you've even dialed.

CONTRIBUTING FROM A COHERENT STATE

Every time the human heart beats, a signal travels out from the body and into the unified field. Scientists have shown that your emotional state, attitude, and thoughts create different signals, which the field broadcasts far and wide. It's very similar to how a radio broadcasts sound through an electromagnetic wave; only humans broadcast their signals as energy with specific signatures or encoded information.

Most people broadcast their signals unconsciously, sending out whatever information is in their unconscious, including their worries and frustrations. But as you practice coherence, you'll learn to broadcast intentionally.

Recently, I spent the weekend with my parents. My dad isn't in very good health, and as my mom was sharing the latest diagnosis from his doctor, it was clear that she was in an incoherent state, experiencing stress around the situation. As she talked, I focused on my heart center, breathing in and out of my chest, and practiced feeling grateful for being there with her. In that moment, I felt grateful that my mom and I have a relationship in which she feels like she can be open with me, because I know not all families have that safety or intimacy. It didn't matter what words were coming out of her mouth; I was grateful that we were sharing that time together in physical form.

After just a few minutes, my mom's whole demeanor shifted. Although she'd started the conversation with flustered energy and an anxious tone of voice, she soon grew calm and present. The lines of worry cleared from her brow, she made eye contact with me, and she stopped fiddling with her hands, something she does when she's feeling stressed. Clearly, she was ready to feel more peace around the situation, instead of looking for someone to blame or feeling sorry for my dad or herself. By the end of the conversation, she was way more centered than when we first began and told me the doctors were doing everything they can.

Without saying anything, I was intentionally broadcasting specific information to contribute peace to my mother's state of being. In other situations, though, I've broadcast this same type of information without meaning to. Just as we discussed in Chapter 3, any feeling you experience contributes to the overall collective consciousness, unconsciously inviting everyone in your field to feel the same way as you.

That's why taking the time to practice coherence each day is anything but selfish. By doing it, you're making a huge impact on all of creation. Coherence is a conscious investment in the unified field, and by practicing it, you're actually in service to the world around you.

Karmically, which would you rather take responsibility for: reactively adding emotional and energetic pollution to the field, or generating and sharing gratitude, appreciation, compassion, and love?

Remember that whoever you're with has the sovereign right to either enjoy the coherent environment you're generating, fight to maintain their discomfort, try to pull you into an incoherent state, or leave. When we hold a coherent state for the purpose of us feeling good, without being attached to the outcome or trying to control or manipulate another person's state, then we allow for the highest and best for all.

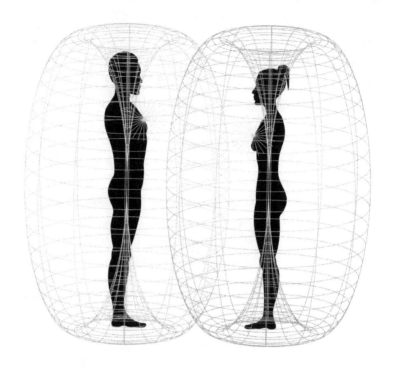

Practicing coherence is your chance to wake up to your own natural empowerment. Coherence allows you to sense your physical body as a tool to support your spiritual growth and increase your level of consciousness. As you draw closer to a state of unity within yourself, you stop feeling disconnected from your highest self and isolated from others, which lessens your feelings of worry, anxiety, depression, craving, regret, and despair. You begin to take caring, loving responsibility for what you contribute to the unified field because you truly feel part of the collective consciousness. While you may not be able to avoid the incoherence of the world around you, instead of trying to avoid it, you can use your own energy field to transmute it, knowing that all words, thoughts, beliefs, and emotions carry a message.

Japanese scientist Dr. Masaru Emoto is known as one of the world's most influential water researchers. His work provides proof that our thoughts, feelings, and intentions affect physical reality. In one of his experiments, he filled glasses with water and taped a piece of paper to the side of each glass. Each piece of paper had a phrase on it—either "I can't stand you" or "I love you"—written in a variety of languages. Along with these phrases, he played different music for the water and enlisted people to speak to the water in different ways: praying over it, yelling horrible things at it, giving the water compliments.

After each information broadcast, Dr. Emoto flash-froze the water to create ice crystals. In the case of positive and high frequency messages, the ice crystals formed gorgeous snowflake shapes with beautiful geometries. In the case of negative and low-frequency messages, the ice crystals formed strange, distorted blobs.

You don't need to be a scientist to tell which crystals are which—they're plain to see. His work showed that each word, thought, belief, or emotion has a specific set of instructions via the electromagnetic field. That's just how the universe works.

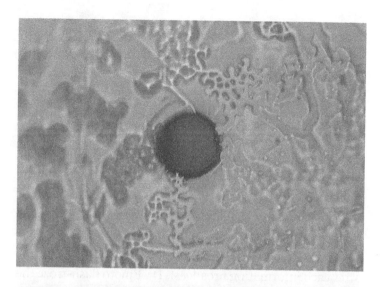

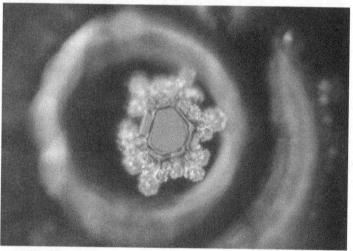

When my son was little, I wrote, "I love you," on the tags of his clothes. After all, our bodies are over 70 percent water—I wanted the water in his body to resonate like the crystals in Dr. Emoto's experiments. To have the same effect on everyone who came into my home, I stuck a Post-it note with the words "I love you, thank you" on all of the five-gallon glass bottles in which our water is delivered. I even made coasters with positive words on them. I still use this system today—I love knowing that the water that my friends and I consume in my home is infused with that energy.

ENERGY LEAKS AND DRAINS

Humans aren't invincible, as much as we might like to think we are. It's part of the human condition to feel emotions and experience situations that don't contribute to coherence. It can seem unavoidable since our culture lives in a habitual state of anxiety, regret, worry, and depression. Naturally, these emotions drain our energy and pull us back toward a perspective that doesn't align with what we truly want to feel. Like draining a battery, these energy leaks deplete our overall life force.

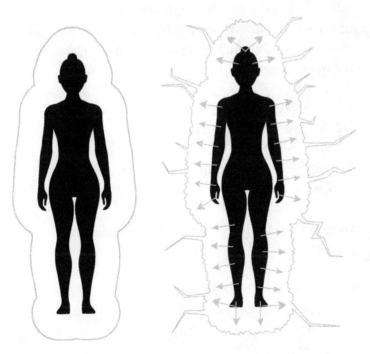

You may have experienced a situation where you wake up feeling great, confident, and at peace, feeling within yourself that all is well. But the second you go out into the world, you start to feel tired and drained. You could blame this on traffic, the people around you, the culture at large, the problems in the world. However, blame is a low-frequency response that only further draws you into an incoherent state. The reality of that situation is that you weren't holding your own energy field in a coherent state. It could have been that you weren't being responsible for your own field, but it could also have been that your best efforts were impaired by an energy leak.

The amazing thing about humans is that we can plug each other's energy leaks. In fact, we're made to do that. The only caveat is that the other person be open to it, even if unconsciously. For example, my mom's goal wasn't to feel bad when talking about my dad and his health. A subconscious part of her wanted to feel peace, which is why she allowed my "broadcast" to flow into her field. As her field expanded, she felt more coherent.

It gets more complicated when one person in a conversation or relationship feels coherent, but the other is uncomfortable with that coherence. If they aren't ready to raise frequency and feel better, that means they are still learning from their incoherent state.

We generally see three options for how this situation can play out:

1. The incoherent person may attempt to pick a fight with the former in a subconscious attempt to lower their frequency and subsequently drop their level of coherence.

This is the misery-loves-company scenario designed to avoid feeling abandoned or alone.

2. The second thing that may happen is that the incoherent one may choose to leave the presence of the coherent one. If they are determined to stay incoherent, they won't be able to maintain that low vibe around a coherent person for long, and they subconsciously know that.

3. The third option is the most fun—it's the same as what I experienced with my mom. The incoherent person allows their field to optimize in response and entrainment with the coherent person's field.

None of these three options are right or wrong, good or bad. They are just experiences that we all have the sovereign right to choose.

WHAT TO DO ABOUT AN ENERGY DRAIN

Humans desire belonging more than almost anything. However, it takes a lot less effort to bring someone down to a lower frequency than rising up to meet their higher one. That's why most situations of collective consciousness end up being energy draining.

When you're the only coherent person in a relationship or a community, you're confronted with a choice of whether to follow the tribal influence of matching others' frequency or to build on the strength and integrity that coherence creates in your energy field. Where others may bring the energy-draining emotions of sarcasm, judgment, fear, and anxiety, you can internally choose reverence, forgiveness, love, excitement, and peace. These are energy-renewing emotions that effectively plug the energy leak.

When you start to take action on your own behalf, the victim-perpetrator-rescuer triangle that is epidemic in our culture begins to break apart. You send the other person a silent message that the unified field is listening, and if they are truly wanting to shift their frequency, they can match the coherence template right in front of them, raise their own frequency, and feel a lot better. Whether or not they take that opportunity, you've made an invaluable contribution to the field by broadcasting your coherence loud and clear.

It's important to bear the unified field in mind even when you're alone. Every time you repeat a story about a time of low frequency, even if it's just going through a memory in your head, your energy system thinks you're living through that state all over again and resends all of that information out into the unified field.

That doesn't mean you can't ever think about the challenging times in your life. Processing those times is a vital part of supporting your healing. However, you have a choice to either let those times become part of the message you continuously broadcast into the unified field or to supersede and transform the events of your past into wisdom and development.

These higher spiritual states are the whole purpose behind our challenges. Again, by practicing coherence, you'll repattern your systems to prioritize energetic messages that align with the highest truth of your heart.

INTUITION

With all this information being broadcast into the unified field, it makes sense that humans would be naturally intuitive. After all, intuition is how we receive and understand the information coming to us from and through the field.

However, it's difficult to act from our intuition in an incoherent state. An incoherent state creates a feeling of separation and isolation, both from others and from the inner/higher self. If you feel separated from your higher self, how can you access and ultimately translate any of the information it's sharing with your conscious mind?

This can be particularly intense when you're in the midst of a challenge. Often, the worst part about a challenge is the feeling of confusion, of not knowing what to do next. Feeling lost, unprepared, and unfamiliar with the situation can tear down your trust in yourself and test your trust in the overall process of life. This activates incoherent emotions like fear and anxiety.

But here's the thing: you can't feel powerless and coherent at the same time. *Feeling coherent equals power.* How amazing is that? Moving into that coherent state makes it so much easier to access the intuition of your sacred heart, which reminds you of your naturally empowered state.

There are various techniques to access intuition, but one of my favorites is to write down whatever you want to access your intuition around, then move into a coherent state and physically put your hand on your heart. Then ask your heart for the highest level of truth in any situation or issue. It takes just ten minutes to do, and 99 percent of the time, it will help you access a higher level of truth. You may not know the entire answer start to finish, but you will know the next step. More importantly, by expanding your consciousness in this way, you'll feel a sense of power that you may not have ever experienced before.

A NEW NORMAL

I said in the beginning that I used to be addicted to incoherence. (I experienced it in the form of problem-solving; as long as I had something to work on I felt relatively normal.) At the same time, I was open to shifting. I didn't have the language for it at the time, but I was magnetically drawn to the coherence I saw in people like Brother Bob.

At this point in my life, I can say that I'm "addicted" to being in a coherent state. How could I not be? It feels natural, free, peaceful, powerful. Whereas before incoherence felt normal and familiar, today it doesn't take much incoherence for me to feel extremely uncomfortable. Because I know that I have a choice about how to feel in any given situation, my tolerance for incoherence has decreased dramatically. If my circumstances cause me to feel a hint of frustration, I activate that choice by turning it off immediately. Instead of letting a situation determine how I'm going to feel, I first observe the situation as a neutral, compassionate witness. When I activate the neutral observer within, nothing has to be pushed, forced, or changed. As a result, I don't have a textbook stress reaction when I feel inner pressure, anxiety, or constriction.

I observe myself and my reactions, honoring whatever comes up. Then I make a conscious choice about how I want to feel. My choice is to feel grateful 100 percent of the time, even if I'm feeling grateful for the opportunity to problem-solve or feeling grateful that I'm honoring my feelings.

This choice factor within coherence is the most powerful part. I realize that I don't have to depend on anyone or anything for how I want to feel and move through life. I am a cocreator of my world, and in fact, living authentically from the heart is the greatest contribution any of us can make to the world.

THE ESSENCE

I lead my students through an exercise in which I encourage them to create a mission statement for their life. It supports them in choosing what they want to contribute to the world during this lifetime, and helps them hold themselves accountable for the energetic signature they are putting into the unified field. Instead of judging yourself for times when you were projecting something low vibe, you wake up to your own power.

Most of us are conditioned to not feel or know what's authentic to us. We know what's familiar to us, our families and our cultures, but we lose touch with what is really true for us, what brings us deeply personal joy.

The strange but wonderful truth is that expressing our individualized nature more fully doesn't divide us, but it actually creates a greater state of unity. We're best able to honor a sense of oneness and connection in humanity as we tune into our own individual expression of the divine. I believe Brother Bob knew this, and that's why he looked at me and everyone else with love and gratitude, and not an ounce of judgment. He saw each person as a unique, individual blessing, and we got the sense that he wanted nothing from us except for us to be who we were.

Your authentic self is a special gift to the planet. Just you being here is a unique, energetic signature. So as you practice creating coherence, notice the places where authenticity is starting to wake up inside of you. Finding your authenticity is the first step to becoming a conscious creator who can help awaken others.

There's a reason your soul chose to bring you here, right now, in this time and place. You have an important contribution to make, one that stems from your authentic individual nature. It's certainly an option to avoid everything dark, ugly, and toxic happening in the world—if that's what you think you're here to do. But the more likely option is that you're here as a force to help tip the scale toward love and to anchor light on the planet. Letting yourself be here, fully authentic and coherent, will keep you motivated to bring your divine spirit into action.

CHAPTER 5

STEP 1

FOOD AND DRINK

While most people think the process of raising conscious-ness is spiritual and energetic only, it's actually a biospiritual process, which also includes the physical, mental, and emo-tional. That means the physical body can help propel spiritual development. What we choose to put into our bodies directly influences our body's frequency, which in turn influences our spiritual awareness.

That said, I know that the subject of food can be a big trigger for some people. However, my mission with this book is to help you on the journey of expanding your awareness. In that effort, it's helpful to realize that what you eat and drink can either activate your spiritual awakening or slow your spiritual development. As we talk about food, know that it's not with the intention of creating judgment toward yourself or anyone else. It's not about weight, appearance, or "eating clean." It's about using food as a gateway to higher consciousness.

That's why, as you read through this chapter, I encourage

you to approach it from your heart center. Abiding in your heart center enables you to release judgment and the instinct for self-protection, allowing you to build empathic energy and curiosity.

CHALLENGES WITH FOOD AND FREQUENCY

At the beginning of Chapter 3, we talked about how the food that is medicine for one person can be poison for another. Like everything else in nature, our food and drink has a certain frequency depending on where it came from, how it was made, what was programmed into it initially, and what other frequencies it encountered on its journey to our plates.

As an awakening being, when you eat things with a lower vibrational frequency, you'll likely experience some disharmony or inner conflict. In contrast, when ingesting high-vibrational food, it becomes easier to connect with higher vibrational energies and beings, such as your sacred heart—your highest and purest guides in spirit and your highest self.

As humans, we often make choices based on the dualities we perceive in a given moment. This duality conditioning has taught us to assign different meanings for different foods, depending on where and how we encounter them. Perceiving a food through a duality lens (as good or bad) can complicate our ability to make intentional, conscious choices around it.

It doesn't help that most humans are conditioned to be unconsciously attracted to lower frequency things, not only in regard to food itself but also to the conditioning around it. As a result of this tendency, there are a number of typical challenges you might encounter as you shift into more consciousness around the food you consume.

CHALLENGE 1: SYMBOLISM

The human brain tends to favor the shorthand of symbolism for making choices. However, each symbol only has the meaning which we individually assign to it or collectively agree to.

The swastika is an excellent example of this. These days, most of us associate a swastika symbol with Nazi Germany. However, for over 5,000 years before that era, the same symbol was a widely used symbol for good fortune and prosperity among the ancient and modern world, including Egypt, India, Europe, China, Japan, and North America. The word itself comes from the Sanskrit *svastika*, meaning "conducive to well-being."

The same stark difference can be true with food. Take cake and champagne as an example. Nutritionally, neither is the healthiest option for you or your body. However, cake and champagne are both tied to a sense of celebration in Western culture. Chances are that if you're consuming these foods, you're in a state of high frequency, surrounded with love, happiness, and excitement. For some people, the high-frequency context of celebration can help prevent an unwanted reaction to these foods.

Meanwhile, for others, even those who aren't physically sensitive to the ingredients, even the smell of cake and just a sip of champagne might trigger an uncomfortable physical response because of some past conditioning or trauma from an event where they were served (a funeral reception for example, or a party that didn't end well for you), in addition to the overall frequency differential.

That's why it's helpful to recognize what certain foods symbolize to *you*. Free yourself from the cultural connotations of foods and focus on your own interpretation. By doing so, you begin moving into a place of activating your free will around food instead of living by default.

CHALLENGE 2: TRIBALISM

Food and drink are powerful tools of tribal belonging, helping you feel connected with family and friends. When you go to your parents' home for a visit and everyone is eating the same foods they've always eaten, it may be easy for you to join in, even if you wouldn't typically eat that way. Not only do you want to share in an experience that reminds you of your childhood, but subconsciously, you don't want to raise your frequency so much that you'd feel isolated from the people around you.

Earlier in my life, my mom would often roast a turducken, jambalaya stuffed into a chicken stuffed into a duck stuffed into a turkey. This is a common holiday dish in Louisiana, and for a long time, the smell would remind me of home, giving me a sense of comfort, safety, and community.

Today, though, I bring my own food to my parents' house for the holidays. The smell and taste of those foods no longer symbolize love and belonging to me, but they don't symbolize judgment or superiority either. I moved through those interpretations in the process of shifting into higher frequency ranges but eventually arrived at a place where I honor my family's choices. Everyone has a right to live however they choose, and I respect the fact that some of my family still lives within that energy field. We all shift according to our karmic curriculum in our own divine timing.

Meanwhile, even though I'm choosing to eat something different from everyone else, I don't feel left out. Instead, I feel grateful to be there, surrounded by the energy of love and family. I'm tuning in beyond the tribal energies of sameness and allowing love to overlight my perception.

CHALLENGE 3: DEPRIVATION AND SIMPLICITY

When we're talking about food, and diets in particular, it's common to simply focus on what is off limits. Others fall into the trap of following popular diets simply because they offer clear, unambiguous guidelines: here's what you can eat and here's what you can't.

But the choice to follow a popular diet just because everyone else is following it, or because it's simple and takes the guesswork out of eating, is *not* an example of accessing your intuition. If your goal is to raise frequency, it's all about choosing foods that support your biospiritual process and finding the simplicity in that.

CHALLENGE 4: PAST CONDITIONING OF SUPERIOR/INFERIOR

Say you choose not to ingest a food because of how it affects you energetically. Making a conscious choice is great, but the frequency shift of that choice can be negated if you simultaneously project energies like judgment, fear, and frustration toward the people in your life who do eat that food. In that case, you're still living according to old conditioning but from a position of superiority. When you choose to eat "good" food based on underlying conditioning, you actually lower its frequency, and subsequently your frequency, with your judgment.

Just noticing the judgment that comes up within you allows you to begin to move out of the low-vibe conditioning around food that may have accompanied you for a long time. That's the truly challenging part of selecting foods because it requires an intention of self-love and discernment without judgment.

CHALLENGE 5: HASTE

As your frequency rises, you might find that you can no longer tolerate lower vibration foods. When you ingest something that isn't aligned with your energetic template, your physical/energetic body will match the frequency by either rising or falling, depending on the situation. As we talked about in the previous chapter, this shift is typically accompanied by discomfort.

Understandably, someone might get really sick if they're only eating processed food. However, if that person suddenly starts eating a raw organic diet, they might feel just as bad (or worse). That disharmony is the result of a sudden transition rather than a gradual one. Whenever you haven't acclimated to the vibration of the food you're ingesting, you're likely to experience some unwanted side effects, regardless of the body's need for the nutrients.

On the whole, if your goal is to achieve a high level of consciousness, it makes sense to choose foods with higher vibrations. However, keep in mind that a sudden shift in frequency may create some disturbances in the brain and body. Gradual transitions are more comfortable in the short run than sudden shifts.

I know it can seem complicated. That's why it's important to remember that the effect of certain foods is different for each individual. Moreover, your interpretations will change over time. Changing symbolism is simply a process of moving out of the program you were given and making a conscious choice based on the experience you want to have.

THE SUFFERING OF NONHUMAN ANIMALS

When we look at living beings in the context of our overall belief system, there's a cultural belief system of hierarchy. Some living beings are given more value than others, worthy of the opportunity to sustain their own lives. This is an extremely slippery slope.

In the past, the practice of slavery was widely considered normal, natural, and totally acceptable for humans to be enslaved and to be seen as less worthy than nonenslaved humans. For a long time, it's been widely accepted for heterosexuals to have more rights than homosexuals, and for male votes to count before females. As recently as 1974, women weren't able to apply for a credit card on their own, in the US. All of those situations, which we see as brutal and unjust today, were considered normal at the time.

It's helpful to consider past cultural conditioning to gain an understanding of how humans have evolved and will continue to evolve in the future. Part of human evolution means that we wake up to the programs around and within us, and begin making conscious choices instead. There's a spiritual impact to being the cause of someone else's suffering, especially when this suffering is intentional. As you grow more intuitive, you naturally become more aware of the hierarchies which humanity has imposed on the natural world.

Here's an extreme example. Imagine you witness your neighbor abusing their child. At first, you might not want to get involved. However, from the time you see the crime taking place, choosing to ignore the situation is choosing to stay in denial, as well as initiating deep inner conflict. It's one thing to not know you're hurting someone; it's another to know you're causing pain and choose not to do anything about it. Once you're aware and able to make a conscious choice, that's where your karmic curriculum comes into play.

I say all this to help frame the often contentious discussion around eating animal products. In Dr. Melanie Joy's book *Why We Love Dogs, Eat Pigs, and Wear Cows: An Introduction to Carnism*, she includes a helpful explanation of how eating meat is a choice borne of ideology rather than a necessity, as it's often depicted.

> Because carnism is invisible, people rarely realize that eating animals is a choice rather than a given. People typically don't think about why they eat certain animals but not others, or why they eat animals at all. When eating animals is not a necessity, which is the case for most people in the world today, then it's a choice. Choices stem from beliefs. Carnism is sustained by complex psychological and social mecha-

nisms that cause us to unknowingly act against our core values, our own interests, and the interests of others.[2]

Dr. Joy also talks about how we cannot have free choice without awareness and offers interesting information to help readers recognize their own conditioning. For example, some cultures eat cats and dogs, but most Western cultures consider this appalling. Why this arbitrary judgment? Why are we disgusted that some cultures eat cats and dogs, but not disgusted when our culture eats cows and pigs? Who decided this hierarchy?

As we've already discussed, humans have deep ties to low-frequency things, stemming from symbolism, tribalism, and the unwillingness to take responsibility for another being's suffering.

Interestingly, young children (who tend to have a much higher frequency than adults) often find eating meat much more offensive and don't hesitate to point it out. Recently, I was speaking to a four-year-old boy about bacon. When I explained bacon came from pigs, the boy said, "But I don't want to hurt animals. I love animals."

His dad quickly explained that the bacon came from a store—the family didn't hurt the animal themselves.

"But didn't someone have to hurt the pig to get the bacon?" the boy questioned.

A child's vibration is often such that they simply aren't will-

---

2   Melanie Joy, *Why We Love Dogs, Eat Pigs, and Wear Cows: An Introduction to Carnism* (Newburyport, Massachusetts: Conari Press, 2009).

ing to participate at any level in murder, torture, or abuse of animals. They subconsciously know that paying someone to kill an animal holds the same energy as killing the animal themselves. They feel a stronger sense of connection with their Divine Source and so are not afraid to feel a responsibility for how their actions impact the world.

That's what it's like to live at a high frequency. You feel empowered by responsibility, not burdened by it. Choice is freedom. Conditioning has caused people to feel chronically disempowered by our governments, corporations, money, jobs, relationships, and even our own bodies. For this reason, adults frequently repress the inner conflict around an issue like animal suffering. It's less burdensome, and more culturally acceptable, to go along with the majority.

Personally, I don't remember exactly when I made the connection between animal products in food and actual animals, whom I've always loved. However, I do distinctly remember a girl in high school who didn't eat animal products. *How is she surviving while everybody else eats?* I wondered, struggling to get my head around the isolation I believed she must feel. It never occurred to me that she might feel happy, free, and natural (not to mention *not* starving to death) for making that conscious choice.

My decision to stop eating animal products didn't happen until a dream I had later in life. In the dream, I was sitting at a round table with all of my guides in spirit. There was a chicken breast on the plate in front of me. As I put a knife and fork in it, blood splattered out. Eyes of terror looked out at me. I pushed myself back from the table.

In a panic, I asked the guide on my right, "What's going on?" He asked if I'd be willing to kill the chicken myself. I shook my head no. He pointed out that I was willing to pay someone else to kill it. What was the difference between supporting other people who kill and killing an animal myself?

Together, we looked at my fingernails, which I keep really short. Then he showed me an image of a tiger with long teeth and claws. "Don't you think you'd have longer nails if you were meant to eat this way?" he asked. "Don't you think you'd have longer and sharper teeth?"

To say that dream was traumatic would be a major understatement. I felt sick. Since then, I haven't eaten an animal product or bought any animal-based clothing. I've seen the suffering animals go through, and I choose not to be aligned with it. My guide helped me realize that the inner conflict I was experiencing around eating animals wasn't sustainable. I needed to align my heart and my soul with my actions.

THE FOOD WE CONSUME CONSUMES US

So many people are fixated on gaining and losing weight, avoiding allergies, rewarding themselves, or fitting in with their tribe that they never stop to acknowledge the truth that whatever we physically consume also requires energy from us.

Every living being incarnates with an original divine blueprint, the foundation for our soul curriculum. It's an all-encompassing physical/emotional/mental/energetic software program designed specifically for each being. Whatever you choose to eat means taking that being's blueprint into yourself. Either you have to process it by incorporating it into your own soul curriculum or process it by getting rid of it.

When you eat an organic apple, there's an energy which causes it to align with your natural blueprint. It becomes part of you and impacts how your body optimizes. In most cases, any low frequencies that might have impacted this apple are a small percentage compared to the high frequency it carries from being pure, simple, organic, and unprocessed. This is beneficial and easy for you to incorporate into your own blueprint.

Now imagine ingesting anything which has its own specific consciousness. Its divine blueprint can't align with yours— it's like trying to run a post office's software code on a retail clothing store system. These programs aren't made for the same purpose, so they won't align.

Furthermore, ingesting that animal means that its nature will also become a part of you. Imagine the animal came from a factory farm (most do) where the environment caused the animal to feel stressed, anxious, overwhelmed, hopeless, shocked, and lonely. By eating that animal, you're inviting in all these emotions which aren't aligned with your original blueprint. Eventually, that will express itself in some way and exert an influence.

It's not a coincidence that so many vegans eventually resonate with relatively peaceful energy. Not eating animals plays a major role in the culture of nonviolence. Even if animal torture wasn't the point for them eating a vegan diet, eventually the lack of "torture energy" ingested in their bodies facilitates more peace, if they allow it.

For some reason, carnivores love to ask me what I'd do if I were on a deserted island where my survival depended on eating meat. Would I really rather starve to death than kill and eat an animal? I like to respond to that question with another question: Do you feel like you already have enough anxieties, traumas, and fears, or do you really want to amplify what's already on your karmic plate by consuming more of that trauma energy?

My priority is to honor and respect all living things, including animals, trees, and plants, and I do the best that I can. Any animal has the same right to survival as I do. I don't want to prioritize my survival over a nonhuman animal's, especially when we have the same qualities of emotion and priorities of family dynamics, loyalties, love, and allegiances.

When I was last asked that question, I answered that I'd eat plants and berries until I couldn't anymore. If I died there, I'd die there. Their response was, "The animals would eat you because they don't care about you the way you care about them."

And you know what? That may be true. But as Gandhi argues, man's supremacy over lower animals doesn't mean that the former should prey on the latter. Instead, it means the higher is intended to protect the lower. It's natural to have mutual aid between the two, as there is between one human and another.

"The greatness of a nation and its moral progress can be judged by the way its animals are treated."
—MAHATMA GANDHI

Even if we don't say anything aloud, we're often making excuses for our culture. Just because it's the way things have always been done, that doesn't make it right. That little voice in the back of our minds can be one of the most disempowering and deconstructive energies.

Essentially, you're giving up. You're saying you don't have another choice but to conform.

Another question that I hear often is about whether plants feel pain when they are harvested for food. Why don't I feel bad for hurting the plants? The answer is that plants don't have pain receptors, a brain, or a central nervous system. As a result, it's actually impossible for them to feel pain. The evolutionary process of human and nonhuman animals has allowed for the central nervous system to alert us to pain so we can escape a potentially life-threatening situation, something that plants cannot do since they cannot run. If they were equipped with pain receptors, evolution would ensure that they were also outfitted with mobility.

Plants definitely react to energy, but they don't respond to energy like human and nonhuman animals do. For instance, they have automated reactions to love and fear, though they don't process that love and fear in the way that human and nonhuman animals do.

If someone is fully invested in the "plants feel pain" theory, it's interesting to consider that it takes up to thirty-five pounds of plants to create just two pounds of nonhuman animal flesh. In other words, a carnivorous diet would theoretically produce far more plant pain than a vegan one.

One of the best resources for exploring the nuances of plant-based eating is vegan educator Earthling Ed. We've included a shortlist of our favorite selections from his content in the Resources section at the end of this book.

Remember that the physical body is designed to be a tool for consciousness expansion. It was designed to support the whole evolutionary process, not for you to drag it along throughout your life or for it to be a burden. Throughout your entire spiritual journey, you'll learn to use your body as a tool. You'll understand how to fuel it and plug it into supercharged higher frequencies instead of feeling like it's dragging you down.

When you learn how to properly fuel your body, all of the systems—your lightbody, energy body, and emotional, physical, and mental aspects—start working together without discord or inner conflict. Everything starts working together in a harmonious state. You discover a newfound lust for life. Regardless of your age or physical condition, you experience vitality like you possibly never have before. You're in a state of universal flow, which is where deep spiritual development begins. It doesn't matter if you can't run five miles or if you aren't in as good of shape as you were when you were twenty. An Olympic athlete can be in perfect shape and still feel constriction. In a flow state, you can transcend the limits of your physical body because your systems are working together. The meaning of the word "diet" becomes clear. No matter your physical circumstances, you feel total freedom and liberation. You feel truly alive, able to thrive, not just survive.

TAKING RESPONSIBILITY

After the traumatic dream I described, I went through a pretty intense emotional detoxification. I experienced a lot of self-judgment and grief. When I came out of denial, I couldn't believe I hadn't looked at eating meat and dairy that way before. I actually cried a lot in the first few months because I was processing my feelings of shame and sadness. I had spent years giving away my own power and self-authority. In the past, I was more concerned with not eating too many carbs than the impact I was having by eating animals and animal products. This was a perceived sense of safety, but I wasn't acting in a way which was fully aligned with my heart. I was asleep to my own inner imbalance. I'm a prime example of somebody who had high levels of consciousness in some areas of my life and lower levels of consciousness in others.

After that dream, I allowed for some time to grieve and ask for forgiveness from the animal kingdom, as well as moving into forgiving myself. I tuned into the collective soul of cows and pigs, wanting to make amends karmically. I couldn't undo what I'd already done, but I wanted to make some sort of shift. I no longer want to contribute to killing of any kind.

Once you wake up to your past resonance with the abuse or killing of other beings, going back to sleep isn't an option.

I learned that making amends with animals is about taking care of them when we can. I began by feeding the birds. Even the process of laying out food and water for birds was highly emotional for me. At first, it seemed like a lame attempt to say, "I'm sorry." It was colored by self-judgment and self-criticism.

I never verbalized any of my judgment, but I did spend a little while feeling judgmental whenever anyone would justify their dietary choices when they were eating animals and dairy, or buying animal-based clothing. My conflict was exclusively internal; I had a lot of trouble respecting their choice. How could they still willingly eat animals, knowing how much abuse they were causing?

Eventually, I recognized that I was only putting myself in a superior position because I was still processing the inferior position. Part of me still lacked forgiveness and an understanding of human evolution. I challenged myself to move back into a phase of unconditional love and understanding. I knew I could decide within my own life what to support according to what felt aligned with my views. My harmony was personal to *me*.

After a year of not eating animal products, I experienced another period of detoxification, where the grief started to resurface. I've heard similar experiences from other people who underwent the same shift in their physical diet—for some, it didn't manifest as emotions but as physical symptoms of pain (old injuries acting up) or as sudden strong cravings for low-frequency food and animal products.

This happens because the body is moving through detoxification on every level. The cells are moving into higher frequency. The lower frequency part of you might well be scared by the idea of moving into an unfamiliar frequency range. This is actually a good sign—moving into a coherent state involves clearing old energies, thoughts, forms, and patterns. As your frequency rises, your body volunteers those energies up to your consciousness for healing. If you stay the course and don't reanchor into that old pattern of lower frequency, that pattern is allowed to transform and be released.

In some cases, you might want to slow down your spiritual growth. Maybe you feel like your intuitive awakening and spiritual activation is out of control. You might get scared and crave things which will slow your transformation. That's okay—it just means that you're taking it at your own pace in your perfect divine timing. You can find support for all aspects of your shift in our online community at RawSpirituality.com.

No part of the Third Eye Diet is about restriction or constriction. It's about an expanded ability and opportunity to love. By making conscious choices about what you ingest, you're expanding your abilities and opportunities to love. You give yourself a chance to feel full of fresh energy without any sort of guilt or shame. Today, I don't have to shut down, numb out, or repress any discordant feelings of harm, abuse, or disempowerment. That is freedom.

WATER

With all the emphasis on food, people often neglect the crucial importance of water they drink. Water is a living organism even when it's ingested. This makes its frequency particularly potent in how it impacts yours.

Have you ever drunk water and felt thirstier? It's not all in your head. Often, when water goes through treatment, the energetic and physically nutritious properties are removed. The pH changes, the natural purity is changed with chemical additives like chlorine and fluoride, and even the water's crystalline structure is disrupted. While this makes the water safer bacteria-wise, it also deadens the vitality the water had in its natural state.

Fluoride in particular is a problem for consciousness expansion. Despite being officially classified as a neurotoxin in the *Lancet Medical Journal*, fluoride is added to all tap water in the US and is even included in everyday things like toothpaste. Studies have found links between the consumption of fluoride and Alzheimer's disease. It also disturbs melatonin production, which then disrupts the body's system around sleep cycles, fat regulation, and hormone balance. Nevertheless, the US medical system prescribes an alarming number of fluoride-based drugs and antibiotics, which have proven to cause permanent neurological damage to many people who use them. Along with poor circulation, organ dysfunction, and inability to lose weight, chronic users of fluoride-based drugs report issues like mood disorders, problems focusing, disorientation and disequilibrium, and intuitive, creative, and mental blocks—all issues having to do with the third eye. It's no coincidence—fluoride toxicity specifically causes calcification of the pineal gland.

When water is flowing in a stream, moving over stones, and twisting around bends, the molecules within the water align themselves with the electromagnetic poles of the planet. The electromagnetic charge within those molecules responds by holding the "memory" of where it has been and what happened on its journey. Just like humans and other living beings, water is changed by its environment.

In Chapter 4, we talked about the experiments of Dr. Emoto, which showed how the actual ice crystals within the water changed in response to various languages, music, and other positive and negative stimuli. In another of Dr. Emoto's experiments, participants prayed over polluted bodies of water. Then researchers measured the contaminant level in both lakes over time and found that the contaminant levels lowered. Proximity made little difference.

Interestingly, it made little difference whether the participants were standing over the body of water, or prayed from many miles away. This illustrates again that time and space are not barriers to the movement of information in the quantum field. All movement of information is vibrational expression.

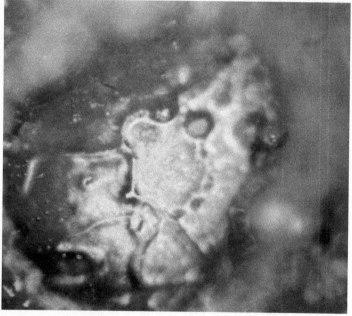

Before Fujiwara Dam

After Fujiwara Dam

For that reason, you want the water you're drinking to help raise your frequency. The first step is to drink the highest vibrational water to begin with. I recommend drinking spring water, since it is closer to its natural state and helps to decalcify the pineal gland. We have ours delivered in glass bottles to avoid plastic leaching more chemicals into the water.

If that option isn't available (and even if it is), you can also elevate your water by radiating a coherent state. By including the water you're going to drink in your coherent field, you can actually restructure its properties. For example, before I eat or drink anything, I put it in front of my heart center. I express my appreciation and allow the waves from my coherent field to pass through the food or water. This creates a harmonious relationship between myself and whatever I ingest. I don't have to waste any energy raising or lowering frequencies if what I consume is aligned with my field. I'm lightening the overall load for my physical and energetic body.

Doing this also creates a sense of appreciation and honor for the food and drink in front of me. I love taking the time to express gratitude before ingesting anything. Eating and drinking are naturally mindful processes. After all, the more you pay grateful attention to something, the more you enjoy it and the better you feel.

RITUALS

Humans love rituals, and food and drink provide natural opportunities for ritual in our lives. Two of the most culturally sacred rituals are the morning cup of coffee and the evening cocktail, beer, or glass of wine.

It's beautiful to have rituals, especially if they help you feel aligned and ready for the day ahead. However, it's common for old souls/indigos/lightworkers/starseeds to start feeling much more sensitive to caffeine and alcohol as they begin to raise their frequency.

Sensitivity to caffeine typically shows up in heart palpitations, insomnia, or feeling on edge, while sensitivity to alcohol may look like an inability to stabilize emotions or to quickly recover from even just one drink. At that point, some people may feel they have to choose between giving up an enjoyable ritual or living with the unpleasant side effects of low-frequency intake fighting the higher frequency they're attempting to create.

In reality, it's not about the drink itself. What matters most is your intention. Rather than agonizing over the decision about whether to drink a cup of coffee in the morning or have a beer with your friends after work, and falling into deprivation-based inner dialogue, ask yourself this: Are you waking up in the morning and drinking coffee because it's a habit or because you're truly and consciously enjoying the ritual and its effects? If you're truly enjoying the ritual but not the aftereffects, you can replace the food/drink with a higher-frequency alternative and still get the joy from the ritual itself.

One of my clients shared with me that when he gets home from work, the very first thing he does is pour himself a glass of wine. It's a ritual for him: he gets home, puts his feet up, relaxes with a drink, and then gets on with the rest of his evening. He realized that his frequency was being blocked by how strictly he adhered to the program he'd created for himself. It's not like he came home, put down his stuff, took a breath, and evaluated whether he wanted something to eat or drink. Instead, the glass of wine was an automatic behavior rather than a conscious decision.

The intention behind the way you drink these ritualistic beverages makes a huge difference in how they affect your intuitive process.

Choosing to ingest these beverages isn't a matter of right or wrong any more than a certain food is good or bad. Rather, it's a matter of assessing how much energy they require from you and whether you'll decide you'd prefer to use that energy for other purposes. Since caffeine and alcohol are water-based, it's certainly possible to use coherence to enliven and shift the frequency of these drinks. It's wonderful to discover that a mindless habit can be transformed into an opportunity for mindfulness, appreciation, and a coherent state.

It's true that any toxin lowers frequency in your body, which lowers overall vibration. Specifically, caffeine or alcohol can create stress on the nervous system, which causes a lack of focus in meditation and adds more distractions to life. For those who use their coffee as a crutch for adrenal exhaustion or who drink alcohol to wash away the stresses of the day, they typically have little energy left for developing higher levels of awareness. Both our physical and energetic bodies exert a huge amount of energy when purifying these toxins from our system and rebalancing our energies.

WAYS TO RAISE FREQUENCY IN YOUR DIET

Raising frequency through your food and drink is simple, though it's not merely a matter of shopping for organic groceries. That's a great place to start since organic food is as chemical-free as we have access to (grown without insecticides, fumigants, fungicides, herbicides, or carcinogens) and has an average of 30 percent more nutrition than nonorganic food. It's also helpful to eat foods that are as close to their natural state as possible, which includes locally grown produce available in season.

But remember, anything you ingest comes with an imprint.

If you're eating a plant, where was that plant grown? Was it sprayed with something of a low frequency? How was it shipped from one place to another? What did it absorb throughout the shipping process? Where has it been waiting for you to buy it? Every stage of food production leaves an energetic imprint on the food you eventually ingest.

Obviously, you won't typically know every detail of your food's imprint. By the time it gets to you, it might be imprinted with the energies of greed and overwhelm from the people who stored it, for example. Fortunately, we have the ability to purify the energetic imprints of foods before we ingest them through our coherent, deeply grateful attention.

In addition, there are a number of specific foods that offer great benefits for opening the third eye and supporting your spiritual and intuitive awakening.

- **Raw organic cacao.** If you love chocolate like I do, unroasted cocoa beans is a delicious, high-vibe version that, when eaten in moderation, provides healthy stimulation to the pineal gland.
- **Spirulina and blue-green algae.** Both these foods are great for stimulating the pineal gland. Do your homework to ensure it's from clean, nontoxic sources. I like E3 Blue Majik Certified Organic Spirulina. Because it is mechanically extracted, it has no stabilizers, chemicals, or excipients.
- **Turmeric.** This bright golden rhizome has great anti-inflammatory properties.
- **Ginseng.** If you are particularly sensitive to caffeine, ginseng can offer an energy boost while helping raise your physical body's frequency.

- Coconut oil. This is generally great for the brain and specifically for the pineal gland.

The amount that you eat is just as important as the food itself. Whenever we eat more than our digestive system can handle, we overload the system, which creates stagnation and slows down our spiritual and intuitive acceleration. All of our energy goes toward digestion instead of the energetic restructuring and expansion that our lightbody must undergo in this awakening process.

BLESSING YOUR FOOD

We talked in the previous chapter about how coherence begins with gratitude. This is especially fun to observe in relation to food. Unfortunately, the majority of modern culture has lost the sense of honoring their food. Food is no longer seen as a communion between us and what we're ingesting. We've lost the level of ritual, and instead we eat while driving or looking at our phones.

In contrast, expressing blessing over food is evident in the earliest human cultures. Back then, they had no soapy water or ways to sanitize the tools for preparing and eating food. It's a miracle that humankind still exists through all the bacteria, viruses, pathogens, and fungi it has faced over the centuries.

Many people in traditional cultures bless their food with their hands in the Anjali mudra—the prayer position where the hands are pressed together in front of the heart center. This mudra actually helps to connect the two hemispheres of the brain, creating balance. When you hold your hands in that position, with your thumbs against your chest, the corpus callosum between the brain's hemispheres is activated, beginning a coherence process.

Blessing your food before you eat forces you to slow down, take a breath, and feel grateful for the food, as well as the time and effort that went into preparing it. It's less about the words you say and more about the thoughts and feelings of gratitude and appreciation.

Those feelings create a coherent environment that raises frequency in everything it contains, including the food and drink you're about to consume. When the frequency of your food matches your own high frequency, your system doesn't have to overwork in order to balance things out. In essence, you're preharmonizing your food and your body before anything even physically enters your system.

JUDGMENT VS. DISCERNMENT

Making a transition in your physical diet can be challenging. Along with all the energetic shifts and detoxification that happen along the way, there may be an added element of judgment around your choices. Sometimes, this judgment comes from an external source—friends, family, healthcare providers, or whatever diet information is popular right now.

Other times, though, it can come from your past or your own mind.

The only reason we judge others is because we're scared ourselves. The more you're willing to observe and question that frightened space within yourself, and examine the origins of that fear, the more you will easily move into nonviolence holistically—not just in your actions but also in the food you consume and the systems you support. That's why, no matter what choices you're making right now around food and drink, I encourage you to notice when judgment is surfacing, honor that it's there as a symptom of change, and allow it to release by observing rather than calcifying around it.

There's a big difference between judgment and discernment. Judgment divides concepts, people, and situations into good, bad, right, or wrong. Discernment is about consulting your heart-based intuition and discovering what resonates with you. Intuitive eating and drinking are about taking that moment to focus on the heart center and make a resonant decision from a conscious, orderly, appreciative place. To eat and drink intuitively, you need to take a pause, connect with your highest self, notice your habits around food and drink, and make conscious choices from a coherent state.

It actually takes a lot of energy to hold judgments in place. Often, it can require just as much energy as it takes to balance the effect of toxins you've ingested. Are you ready to free up some of that energy? In this new state, things aren't good or bad—they just are and either resonate with you or they don't. When you let yourself off the hook and stop judging everything, you'll experience a childlike freedom that you may not have even experienced when you were a child!

There are specific mantras and mudras which can facilitate the move from judgment to discernment. One that I like is *"Lokah samastah sukhino bhavantu."* Loosely translated, this means, "May all living beings be happy and free, and may my actions contribute to that happiness and freedom."

THE ESSENCE

While food and drink are far from being the only focus of the Third Eye Diet, in my experience they are a doorway to higher levels of discernment, intuition, and levels of consciousness.

CHAPTER 6

STEP 2

ENVIRONMENT

Before my body was diagnosed as chemically sensitive, my symptoms could easily be written off as stress-related. In alignment with my "keep on, keepin' on" personality, my strategy was to mentally and emotionally minimize my symptoms and do my best to keep moving on.

Notice the differentiation between "I" and "my body." When we honor each aspect of us, we no longer believe that "I am ill" but rather "my body is experiencing an illness." This can be a critical step toward cultivating the neutral witness perspective.

But the longer I ignored my symptoms, the more severe they became. In addition to insomnia, migraines, and joint and muscle pain, I began experiencing intense fatigue, lethargy, mental fog, and confusion. Even basic daily tasks took everything out of me. One day, after walking the two blocks back from my son's school, I became terribly out of breath. I stumbled in the door and had to lie down for a few hours. It took all my energy to get up and take a shower. Afterward, I lay in bed with dripping hair—just the idea of drying it felt like more than I could handle.

By the time I started experiencing heart palpitations, I was already making the rounds to various doctors. This became its own challenge, as every doctor I visited gave my condition a different label: fibromyalgia, chronic fatigue, Lyme disease, rheumatoid arthritis, psychosomatic (i.e., all in my head). I ended up with a stack of diagnoses, none of which could be confirmed through Western medical testing. The one thing my doctors agreed on was that whatever was happening to me, it was happening at a subclinical level, making it undetectable in lab tests.

Then things went from bad to worse. I went from barely being able to climb the three steps in my house to needing help walking to waking up and not being able to move my legs. My then husband had to help me around the house and even wash my hair for me. I remember on one of the darkest days, I asked him to promise to take care of my son if I didn't make it.

On top of everything, my brain fog was so bad that I couldn't look for solutions. I lived in survival mode, just putting one foot in front of the other.

AN ANSWER

By the time I visited the twenty-second doctor, an Italian cardiologist, I was having extreme cardiac issues—my heart missing beats, pain in my chest, dangerously low blood pressure. When he walked in the door, he looked up from the big stack of my files from the previous doctors I'd seen, looked me up and down, and said, "I think I know what's going on with you."

Those were the sweetest words I'd ever heard.

This doctor understood that my heart symptoms were only one piece of the puzzle. It seemed that every system in my body was struggling. He believed that my body was unable to cope with the buildup of toxins from daily life due to a genetic mutation. This was affecting my nervous system and subsequently every system in my body.

Not only did this European cardiologist give me the first glimmer of a true understanding of my body's condition by connecting toxic overload with my physical state, but he referred me to a doctor of osteopathy (DO) whom I've now worked with for almost twenty years.

This DO saved my physical body by helping me discern what puts my body into overload. He's helped me recognize when my bucket is overflowing and when my body's filtration systems aren't effectively disposing of the toxins that I encounter.

I share this story in order to assure anyone who is experiencing similarly mysterious symptoms. What happened within my body is not unique. Many old souls are genetically and energetically predisposed to react to their environment more than the general population. When old souls/lightworkers/starseeds/indigo souls are born, we are descending into the 3D world in physical form from a 5D and above consciousness level. The challenges that old souls often encounter with the environment are a result of the lack of integration of the physical body completely into 3D from the higher dimensions. These challenges can show up as allergies, multiple chemical sensitivities, feeling like you don't belong in the modern world, and other issues related to "fitting in" with the low-vibration earth plane. Resolving this disparity means moving into coherence and integrating it into your everyday way of being.

From a spiritual perspective, before any symptom manifests in your physical body, your energetic/emotional/mental state typically would have been out of balance for some time. Many old souls are born with an already active specific issue (one that wasn't handled in another lifetime), and often these souls have chosen to karmically handle that issue for the higher purpose of healing the physical or emotional manifestation of the pattern. This clears and heals the pattern not just in their own physical/emotional/mental bodies but also both up and down the entire family line.

WHY WOULD I CHOOSE THIS?

As we discussed in Chapter 3, it's common for people to react against the notion that they have somehow chosen an experience of pain, sickness, or suffering. I certainly reacted against it at first. Why would I, on a soul level, choose to be in a situation that would activate such traumatic, near-death experiences?

But as I worked with my DO and began to physically and emotionally heal, I began to wake up to the answer. My soul had chosen this situation so that I could clear and heal the genetic imprints within my lineage and share the methods and healing with my students and clients.

Any experience of suffering will either break you enough to motivate a transition out of this physical lifetime, or it will convert into wisdom which you can then share with others. Either way, a higher-level decision is being made, consciously or not.

Trigger points in people's lives—you meet someone, you encounter something, you arrive at a specific place—activate a soul contract. That contract starts moving on its own trajectory, powered by its own engine. This is a big topic with a lot to learn about. If you want to explore more, visit my website at AlyssaMalehorn.com and check out our Raw Spirituality Podcast.

This work is very important as the frequency of the planet and our bodies shift. As we raise vibration, many of us become more sensitive to our environment and the different triggers within it. And the more of a chemical burden we put on our physical bodies, the more energy gets diverted from our journey into higher awareness and is used instead to filter and purify these toxins.

Imagine you're about to go on an intense hike. Would you want to eat a really heavy meal right before you set out? Probably not—your body would be so busy digesting that you wouldn't have the energy to hike. You'd probably rather curl up on the couch and take a nap.

Environmental toxins work in the same way. When you have a bigger-picture mission of what you want to accomplish in your life, do you really want to fill your physical body up with toxins that it has to purify? Regardless of your genetic predisposition to flush toxins, if you live in a prolonged incoherent state and continue to accumulate impurities from your environment, your body will eventually need to hit pause to catch up. In an incoherent state, all systems in the body are working at a subnatural level, making them even less able to deal with this planet's toxic overload. But if you support a state of coherence by making choices that don't require your body to go into overdrive, you're able to activate a (literal) supernatural level of well-being.

Our physical bodies are simply not designed to detoxify the amount of toxins with which we're consistently flooded in a modern environment. Nevertheless, the challenges with living in an environment like this are so familiar that many folks might not even know what it's like to live within an environment that supports their frequency.

In a frequency-supportive environment, you have the overall emotional feeling that your environment is supportive of *you*. When an environment is frequency modulating, you feel like your environment flows with you, supporting your brain and your heart in remaining coherent. Like an adaptogen, the space around you responds easily to the ways you choose to positively shift it. You feel calm but alert, both safe and inspired. Your subconscious mind is able to relax within a space like this.

Anyone certified in hypnosis and neurolinguistic conditioning knows that your subconscious mind assesses any room you walk into long before your conscious mind observes it. It picks up on the smallest imbalances and puts your subconscious mind on high alert. But by paying attention to how you're affected by your environment, you can move into a space of empowerment.

When we are energetically optimized and coherent, the electromagnetic fields of our physical bodies gain the power to detoxify the environmental issues which exist on the planet. It can take a while for our bodies to evolve to that point, but making adjustments to our environment where we can offers a great opportunity to begin the process.

That's what this chapter is all about—creating harmony within your environment. The more you lighten your toxic load, the less you'll feel burdened by physical life. The more you nourish your third eye through the practices listed in the next section, the more enthusiastic and empowered you'll feel, both in your daily life and in the work of raising your consciousness.

CLEARING UP THE CLUTTER

You've probably had that experience where you're out and about in the world, having a great day, then your mood plummets as soon as you walk into your disorganized house.

Maybe you've even found reasons to stay away from your home because you know that confronting the disorder will bring you down.

What happens when you finally do go home? You might start to feel tired, frustrated, ungrateful, and overwhelmed. The great energy you had during the day starts to plummet. This is a common response to clutter, especially if you're already living primarily in an incoherent state.

To cope with this drop in energy, you might have tried a number of different things to make the situation better. For example, you may have used a synthetic air freshener or lit a scented candle so that at least the room will smell good. However, this kicks your body's filtration systems into over-drive—not only are they trying to detoxify and raise the low frequencies of the room, but now they're also processing the low frequencies, carcinogens, and other toxins from those artificial scents.

At this point, you might make some coffee or eat some sugar as a quick pick-me-up to restore the energy you lost since walking in the door. But now your adrenals are also headed into overload. You find yourself with a bunch of nervous energy, which only heightens your incoherence. Maybe you turn to a distraction, like TV, social media, or a phone call to take your mind off the situation. This, however, only creates more incoherence (as we'll discuss in Chapters 7 and 8).

The issue of clutter has recently come to the forefront of popular attention, thanks to Marie Kondo's book *The Life-Changing Magic of Tidying Up* and *The Home Edit* by Shearer and Teplin. While their work doesn't mention the foundational aspect of frequency, the shifts that happen when you keep items that bring you joy, dispose of items that don't, and organize your space ultimately raises vibration.

As it happens, decluttering a room can be a powerful tool for supporting a coherent state. My recommendation is to start by practicing the heart-focused breathing from Chapter 4 then take everything out of the room (or out of a drawer or closet, whatever your area of focus is). Then begin bringing things back in one by one. As you do this, you'll notice which items knock you out of your coherent state. Only keep things in the room that feel joyful, supportive, or uplifting.

WHAT IF IT DOESN'T HELP?

It's possible that you could make these changes to your environment but not notice any significant shift. In that situation, the issue might be that the changes are not coming from a place of empowered energy. Your physical (outer) environment is in concert with your energetic (inner) environment. In other words, a chaotic desk may *indicate* a chaotic state of mind, but a chaotic desk can also *contribute* to a chaotic state of mind. The good news is that you have the power to make adjustments and shifts in your physical environment to create a situation which will support your inner world. All it takes is awakening your own power within the environment.

Just as with food and drink, creating an intention around your environment is the foundation of shifting frequency. Once you set the intention to become more connected with your highest and most coherent self, you'll naturally feel inspired to upgrade your environment by creating more stability and support.

Even more exciting is how that intention triggers your unconscious to guide your conscious mind to make specific choices. Where you might have felt your energy draining at the sight of all the clutter, your intention can shift that into a motivation to clean up your space.

Where you might have turned to synthetic air fresheners and scented candles, you might instead find yourself not liking those scents anymore and instead being drawn to diffuse a natural essential oil. Although that shift might seem random, it's not. In reality, this move aligns with your intention to raise your frequency. The cocreator within you has awakened, guiding you in ways you may not be fully aware of yet.

FREQUENCY FACTORS IN YOUR ENVIRONMENT

The modern world runs on a number of processes that lower the frequency of our collective environment. This creates a challenge for people that is only going to continue to grow. Identifying these factors typically either creates a low-vibe state of anxiety or overwhelm ("How am I ever going to heal the damage done by my environment?") or a high-frequency state of empowerment ("I consciously choose to make some shifts now.").

As we go through the following list and describe the ways these various factors can affect us, my recommendation is to activate your brain and your heart in a state of coherence. Remember, when you combine a high-vibration intention with a coherent state of heightened emotion, you've remembered and activated your most empowered, natural state.

EMFS

In the past, whenever I had a cell phone anywhere near me, my body felt an uncomfortable buzzing, even when the phone itself wasn't vibrating. My nerves were heightened, and I had a jumpy fight-or-flight response to the smallest things, like a screen door slamming in the wind.

This problem only worsened when Wi-Fi came onto the scene. I knew whenever our Wi-Fi router was on, thanks to the migraines, irritability, and insomnia that it triggered. Every cell in my body struggled to stay in balance with the artificially produced chaotic electromagnetic frequencies emitted by our modern environment.

Discordant electromagnetic frequencies are everywhere in

our modern world. These frequencies move through your physical body, bringing an overabundance of unbalanced information that is incredibly hard for your physical body to translate. Your cells become confused about what to prioritize—*Is it most important to get rid of cancer cells? Should we work to activate the immune system? Should we help balance the emotional state or allow for sleep?* Studies have shown how this confusion creates a carcinogenic impact within the cellular system, among other things. With 5G now part of the equation, the toxic load is heavier than ever, contributing to myriad health issues. For this reason, some countries and many cities have banned 5G.

Some electromagnetic frequency (EMF), Wi-Fi, and 5G exposures also create an additional, little-known side effect: consciousness-lowering waves that have the effect of limiting your spiritual expansion. With these waves broadcast from multiple surrounding sources, you might easily find yourself rehashing the same arguments without resolution, experiencing difficulty accessing will power, feeling easily triggered, controlled by your desires, unable to let go of the past, or stuck as you move through an illness or trauma.

Fortunately, these impacts can be mitigated. One of the primary optimizers that we use is the Focused Life Force Energy (FLFE) mentioned in Chapter 4, which we affectionately refer to as "Fluffy." This service converts the chaotic frequencies of EMFs coming from our cell phones and routers into harmonic waves. You can actually see them in a scientific graph, where they show up as orderly and coherent waves. Our FLFE subscription is beamed into our house, my meditation center, my office, my parents' house, my son's house, and my partner Zack's workplace. We also have it beaming from our cell phones and necklaces, creating a 300-foot radius of high-consciousness fields. The level of consciousness that's broadcast by the FLFE service is the energy of unconditional love.

 I can't recommend the FLFE service enough. As a reminder, you can get a fifteen-day free trial on this service at FLFE.net/alyssa or by using the QR code here. To learn more about FLFE, visit the links in the Resources section at the end of this book.

EMFs are the most recent culprits to frequency disorder in our environment, but they're not the only ones. Radio frequencies can also disrupt the pineal gland's ability to produce melatonin, which regulates the sleep/wake cycle.

CHEMICALS

Way back when my body's chemical sensitivity issues started, we had a new mattress which had been treated with silicate-based flame retardants. We had a new car, which is one of the most toxic places you can find yourself in—think plastic off-gassing, chlorine out-gassing, and all sorts of surface protector treatments. Our house had been sprayed for bugs. We had new carpet.

What we didn't realize back then was that every product, from the carpet to the insulation to the glue under the floor, emits low-frequency chemicals. Some are detectable by smell, but many are not. In the presence of these chemicals, the glands in your body (especially the pineal and pituitary glands in your brain) can become dysregulated. The dysregulation can manifest emotionally as well as physically, slowing you down one minute and speeding you up the next. In my case, sometimes my blood pressure would dip, and my heart rate would feel slow and heavy. The next minute, my heart would be racing, and I'd feel full of anxiety. I felt emotionally fragile a lot of the time—it didn't take much to make me cry.

When the body is in chemical overload, it can create a reaction much like when drunk people get emotional. Over time, trying to keep up with this overload can trigger adrenal exhaustion, which in turn can create estrogen dominance, which can lead to all kinds of emotional and hormonal instability.

LIGHTING

Think about how healthy, relaxed, and balanced you feel after just a few days of camping or staying in a cabin out in nature. This isn't just a result of taking a vacation. When you're waking up with the sunrise, watching the sunset, and spending time beside a campfire, you're nourishing your pineal gland in the way that our evolutionary ancestors used to do. Maybe you notice your intuition become heightened or a greater state of flow. You might experience a sense of unusual connection to the seasons, the animal kingdom, the trees.

You might find your own sleep cycle improving or start waking up at sunrise but still feel incredibly rested.

Our brains are built to thrive under that type of natural lighting. Our modern world presents a stark contrast, with so many different types of artificial lighting that we can't include an exhaustive list here. Regular fluorescent lighting behaves like television, flickering too many times for the eye to typically notice. However, the brain processes every flicker, trying to string together a million little interruptions to make something continuous. This constant interruption makes it more difficult to stay focused on something in the long-term.

This flickering phenomenon is one aspect of what makes it so important to limit screen time for kids. Their brains are in developmental phases of fast development, and researchers have observed how the flickering effect of television and video games affects children's attention span long-term.

This constant flicker also shifts the way your pineal gland interprets light. Instead of getting the balanced, full spectrum of light that comes from the sun or candlelight, you get more of the blue light spectrum. The blue light inhibits the pineal gland's production of melatonin, compromising sleep and overall health.

In some European countries, fluorescent lights are not used in senior care centers, schools, or hospitals because of the stress they cause on the brain and the glands.

There are a number of ways to rectify this situation. I recommend replacing the LED bulbs in your home or office with full-spectrum lighting. For lamps and lights that we keep on during the evening hours, we use bulbs known as melatonin bulbs (using technology created by NASA to support the sleep/wake cycles of astronauts aboard the International Space Station). Before the bulb is turned on, it appears to have a pink or golden tone because it's manufactured to omit the blue wavelength. However, when you turn it on, the light looks like normal, bright-white lighting. It's a great way to live in the modern world and get light whenever you need it, while still nourishing your body and your pineal gland.

In addition, you can add lighting to your environment that closely mimics sunlight or fire light, such as a salt lamp or other amber lights. This warm red light is deeply nourishing to your pineal gland, helping to support our sleep/wake cycle (circadian rhythm). In public places where you can't change the lights from blue to red or amber, it's helpful to wear blue light–filtering glasses if you're going to be there a while.

COLORS

Different colors stimulate different parts of the energy system and brain. For that reason, it's important to pay attention not only to the color of light but also to the colors we surround ourselves with, from the paint on our walls to the color of our furniture and even what we wear.

Depending on what we're shifting karmically, different colors can be really supportive or really challenging for different people. Generally speaking, colors like gold, silver, and white will affect most everyone the same way: building and stabilizing the energy field, supporting the crown and upper energy centers, helping to keep the aura clean and bright.

The variation increases with other colors. For most people, the darker and denser the color they surround themselves with, the lower the frequency. The lighter the color, the higher the frequency. Most of our color choices are based on this property, though we usually don't realize it. We look at a color and think, "Ooh, I like that," or "I'd never wear that color, but I'd love it on my walls." That attraction is usually because frequency of that color is something we're trying to help balance internally. For example, for some, wearing a dark color can help to ground or anchor our energy if we're feeling flighty or ungrounded.

For a long time, I detested the color red. I remember feeling that way just at a moment when it was very popular for people to paint one red accent wall or have a red couch. But the color disturbed me; I couldn't stand to be around it. When I tuned into why red bothered me, I realized it was overstimulating for my root chakra area. Red is the color that corresponds with the energy center at the base of the spine. It has to do with our survival themes: sexual energy, finances, family of origin, and community. For a lot of people, red can support opening a constricted root center, helping them to feel vibrant and powerful.

But because my root center was already open and balanced, the color made me feel blown out and edgy.

At the same time, I was powerfully attracted to almost all shades of blue and purple. I went through a phase where I painted my world in shades of indigo and violet, and wore a lot of sky-blue and aqua clothing. Looking back, it makes perfect sense—that was during a time when I was working on expressing myself, and sky blue nourishes the throat chakra, which helps people express themselves more easily and clearly.

Both of those responses to color were unconscious. I was drawn to the colors through unconscious connection with my conscious intentions to be in balance. This is typical of how most people relate to color—we make the selection based on instinct, feel the effects of that color's frequency, and create a template. Once that pattern is established, we no longer need to consistently fortify our environments with color because we've already integrated that frequency. We may still prefer or enjoy a color, but it won't feel intense or like a compulsion.

This explains why so many people go through phases of different color preferences, from decor to wardrobe to the possessions in their lives. Consciously or not, we're all on a spiritual healing journey.

SOUND

If you live in a busy city, it makes sense that the sounds around you might feel chaotic or overwhelming to your system. However, a lot of people can normalize these sounds. For example, people who are used to living in big cities tend to crave noise in order to move into a coherent state. Sometimes, when city dwellers go out into the country, they have trouble sleeping because it's so quiet. That's not bad or good, just a reminder to notice what sounds have been normalized within your system.

When it comes to environment, we're all different. However, all humans have one thing in common when it comes to sound: we all respond to the power of the human voice. No sound is more healing than the sonic vibration that comes through a human—it's the most healing device we have in terms of sound. This is true even for people who are deaf or hearing impaired. It's not the actual hearing of the sound but the specific vibration the human voice brings to the systems of the body. The same concept has been studied in completely blind people who show enhanced brain activity and cognition when exposed to light.[3]

Because of the healing power of human voices, using mantras can shift the way our DNA, glands, and cells function and actually optimize their expressions. The vibratory movement which happens in the body can also in effect shake off the calcification of the pineal gland.

By giving yourself positive vibratory support, you're consistently laying the foundation to live in a coherent state, even in environments which lack harmony.

---

3   Université de Montréal, "Study with Totally Blind People Shows How Light Helps Activate the Brain," ScienceDaily, October 28, 2013, www.sciencedaily.com/releases/2013/10/131028090408.htm.

Jonathan Goldman is a sound healing pioneer who has been working in his field for over thirty years. In the book he coauthored with Andi Goldman, *The Humming Effect*, he writes about how a simple vibration from humming can wake up specific glands and energies within you. His findings are supported by a study by the Alzheimer's Research and Prevention Foundation, which discovered the following effects from a twelve-minute singing meditation (or *Kirtan Kriya*) using the sounds *Sa Ta Na Ma*:

- Reverses memory loss.
- Increases energy levels.
- Improves sleep quality.
- Upregulates positive genes.
- Downregulates inflammatory genes.
- Reduces stress in patient and caregiver.
- Improves psychological and spiritual well-being.
- Activates significant anatomical areas of the brain.
- Increases telomerase, the rejuvenating enzyme that slows cell aging by 43 percent, the largest increase ever recorded.
- No side effects.

For details on this meditation, visit the Resources section at the end of this book.

A great way to give yourself this support is by humming root sounds, the kind that are found in traditional meditation mantras. For example, *Aum* (or *Om*) is loosely defined as the sound of the creation of the universe. Many yogis or long-time meditators know that after a period of raising frequency and living in a coherent state, some folks start to hear an *Aum* sound in their inner ear. That *Aum* sound is ingrained so deeply in their mind that it comes in waves. Feelings of bliss and oneness accompany this sound. Hearing it enlivens higher energy centers in your body, helping to support and balance the pineal and pituitary glands. If you've experienced a constriction in these glands and your sense of peace hasn't expanded like you want it to, you can use sound to wake that up.

When we *Aum*, we're recreating something which has always naturally been there at a specific frequency. The exact frequency is different for everybody. With *Aum*, we remind our energy body what it sounds like when all is well. For once, we're not suffering or struggling. We're at one with everything around us. An *Aum* is the sound of unity. The more you meditate, the more the *Aum* sound and feeling will become part of your own inner ambient noise. The feeling of connection you get in a meditative state will start to permeate your regular life.

Some people choose to listen to a particular recording of a chant or mantra to benefit from the vibration. For a free recording of the *Aum* mantra to meditate with, visit the free meditation library in our Raw Spirituality Community (at RawSpirituality.com).

METALS

Humans are constantly interacting with metals. For example, most of us have heavy metal residues from nonorganic food in our system. Dental work contributes to having metals circulating in our systems, not to mention metal implants, copper IUDs, and the naturally occurring iron in our blood, and even elements like aluminum and barium (the primary ingredients in chem trails) being added into our air for the purpose of geoengineering and solar radiation management. All these micro bits of metal are creating an antenna effect in our bodies. As a consequence, we become more affected by things like 5G and Wi-Fi, as well as other naturally occurring electromagnetic fields under the earth and unnaturally occurring fields from the skies.

Even if you don't have a high heavy metal content within your body, the abundance of metals in the environments around us impacts our health, our pineal gland, and our spiritual awakening. Steps to detoxify from metals include ingesting chlorophyll-rich foods, spirulina, spring water, and general detoxification to decalcify the pineal gland. (Note: detox of heavy metals is best done under the supervision of a doctor who specializes in this type of protocol. Metals leave the body from muscles to organs to brain, and when it moves through the brain, you need a huge amount of support to see it through, since leaving the detox process incomplete can have long-term consequences.)

PESTICIDES

As humans, it's normal to want to live in an environment that is clean and free from creatures that carry disease, like rodents and insects. However, causing suffering to another being (even one that we don't want in our homes) typically ends up lowering our frequency. This is certainly the case with pesticides. It's easy to see how the chemical makeup of pesticides can impact our physical health as well as the health of the environment. But an even deeper impact comes from intention, i.e., what you bring to the application.

Believe it or not, there are high-frequency ways to deal with these unwelcome visitors in your environment. Essential oils like rosemary, peppermint, and citrus oils that deter pests from entering your space. (The FLFE service mentioned in Chapter 4 also tends to help deter lower-vibe critters from staying in your space.)

If you're dealing with insects that have already invited themselves into your space, you can lovingly command them to leave. As unlikely as this might sound, if you tell the unwelcome visitor to leave from a heart-centered, coherent energy, many times that's all it takes. After all, as living beings, we all inhabit the same field. If I'm in a coherent state and bring an intention to connect with the ants making a trail through my home, I can say (either aloud or quietly in my mind), "Ants, you are living beings, and I honor your right to live. However, this is my space, and it is really important that I keep this space clean and clear because you unknowingly bring in things that are harmful to me and my family. Thank you for leaving immediately."

I completely know that this may sound strange. However, I can tell you that almost every time after making this command and thanking them in advance for relocating, I wake up the next day and the little critters are gone.

Of course, if we're talking about a bug that can be captured and released back into the wild, that's the most efficient way to remove them from your environment. When that's the case, I thank them for visiting and giving me an opportunity to love them and then send them on their way.

You don't have to command your guests to leave out loud. I usually just make sure that I'm in a coherent state, then direct that love and gratitude to the unwelcome visitor. Then I typically tell them they have three opportunities to leave and then, if they don't make a choice to relocate after that, I'll have to send them back to the light. Since I started this practice, I've never had to send one back to the light; they always leave on their own (or they allow themselves to be captured in a jar and released outside).

I realize how big a hurdle dealing with insects can be for some people. Growing up in Louisiana, roaches caused me serious suffering—they're big, they fly around, and you have to shake out your shoes before putting them on to make sure no roaches have been hanging out in there. After years of fearing roaches, I was conditioned to look for a shoe to kill a roach as soon as I saw it.

But as my frequency rose, I realized that this conflicted with my belief that all living beings have a right to their own sovereignty. Difficult as it was, I chose to make a declaration to the roaches in our environment—"I love you, and I know that you serve a purpose even though I may not know exactly what that purpose is. However, I have created a space here that is healthy and clean for humans and dogs. When you come in, you lower the frequency of that environment. I'll give you three opportunities, and eventually, I'll need to send you away, not because I feel like humans and dogs are more important, but because I'm creating a sovereign boundary here, and if you won't honor that boundary, I'll have to enforce it."

Within a few days, roaches stopped showing up, and it's rare that we see one anymore.

Before you try this technique to get rid of pests in your home, consider your conditioning around those animals. Most people's reaction to bugs has to do with fear or lack of control. If that's you, ask yourself where it came from or what might generate that fear. Did you grow up in a home that wasn't safe and sanitary? Did a parent react in fear about pests or shame other people for having them in their home? Dismantling this conditioning through awareness is foundational to having a high-frequency intention around commanding critters to leave.

CRYSTALS

We are all crystalline beings, and each shift we make into higher frequencies and dimensions/perceptions takes us from a more dense state into a more crystalline state. The crystals we find in nature (or more often these days, in a store) are just like us, receivers and transmitters of energy. That's why people use certain types of crystals to absorb low energy or to attract specific energies into their homes or bodies.

Just as you need to wash yourself, it's important to cleanse your crystals from all the energy they're pulling in. Most people soak them in salt water for a few hours, rinse them, and then dry them in the sunlight or moonlight to clear them of dense energies.

But crystals are also living things and have their own energy to transmit. They have consciousness and purpose, and can be programmed or conditioned, just like us. What many people don't realize is that the majority of crystals on the planet were programmed long ago through absorbing eons' worth of conflicting frequencies from the earth and astral planes. While some stones broadcast healing energies, many were hijacked and programmed to transmit other types of frequencies, not always benevolent.

Fortunately, it's easy to cleanse crystals of programming: physically in a saltwater bath and energetically by holding them to your heart, and with a sense of love, respect, and benevolent intention—"I consecrate this stone for support in my healing."

Just like with pesticides, it's important to examine your own conditioning around the desire to own and use a crystal. Clearing that conditioning will raise your frequency so that you can use the crystal to great effect...or perhaps not need it at all. Either way, it will move from the feeling of "I *have* to have this" to preference, which is an expanded, high-vibe freedom energy.

Another question to ask yourself when raising your frequency is whether you need to own the crystal. Are crystals only intended to be useful to the people who can bring them home, or are they cosmically intended to be naturally supportive for all of us on the planet?

It's not that everything we discover in the earth has to stay there. But some things have specific roles they feel aligned with filling. Crystals can do incredible things, but we have to respect where they belong. Crystal beds naturally occur on the planet in specific areas for a specific purpose, almost like acupuncture points on the earth. That's why I generally advocate for leaving crystals in the earth, so they can do their job of supporting all beings and the planet we share.

I used to own a number of crystals that I used in meditation and healing work. One day, I had a feeling that my stones had a message for me. (Not unusual for a psychic.) "Tell me about your history," I said to them. "What do you need and want now?"

As I tuned in, the crystals answered, "We were kidnapped, taken from our home in the earth without being asked, put on a truck, and then in a store where someone makes money from us. We're being called to be back in the ground to do our job of anchoring higher love and stability into the earth."

Although I was surprised, having never thought of that before, I honored their desire by burying the crystals back in the earth and gave thanks for the support they'd given me. I kept just a few individual stones which had said to me, "We feel like we can be of service here, so we'd like to stay."

You don't have to own the crystal to reprogram it and clear its low frequencies. You can do that from anywhere, in the same way that remote healing works, by sending your healing energy via your intention and declaration into the unified field.

FRAGRANCE

Have you ever been in a skin-care store or the cosmetic department at the mall and felt a little high afterward? That effect is due to a combination of synthetic fragrances, formaldehyde, and pesticides (often combined with other factors like synthetic dyes, toxic lighting, and sound). Many stores contain so many chemicals and have so little fresh air, it makes sense that you might feel weird!

This effect is a clue that even the personal products you use have an effect on your vibration and your intuitive awakening. Everything you put on your skin or inhale—perfume, shampoo, deodorant, etc.—gets absorbed into your system, and as you may know, most of these products are highly toxic.

One of the principal sources of toxicity in personal products is fragrance. These scents, which are mostly synthetic but rarely labeled as such, are largely made of industrial waste and consist of anywhere between 200 to 550 chemicals in every fragrance. Most products are required to undergo scientific testing to ascertain how the combination of chemicals interact with each other. However, the 200-plus chemicals within a fragrance have never been tested in this way, for the simple reason that it would require too much time and money to test them all. There are 3,163 chemical ingredients that hide behind the label "fragrance" in products.

The industrial chemical industry is constantly faced with the problem of what to do with the huge volume of potentially hazardous by-products from the chemicals they manufacture. They can either pay to have those by-products disposed of, or they can sell them to a perfume or cosmetic company.

Most of the fragrances are petroleum-based, such as the scents found in dryer sheets, air freshener plug-ins, and commercial perfumes. (Yes, even the super expensive ones.) These oils coat the inside of the mucus membrane in your nose, making you less sensitive to smell. Maybe you've been around someone who sprays way more perfume than necessary. There's a reason for this: the petroleum-based coating has built up in their nose and left them barely being able to smell at all.

As if that weren't enough, many perfumes also have additives which are specifically designed to target the addictive centers of the brain. While using these products once or twice may not cause any sort of reaction except in super sensitive folks like me, the toxins they contain bioaccumulate, or build up over time. You may have used a product for years without ever having an unpleasant reaction, until one day, your filtration system couldn't handle it anymore, and your body was triggered.

Reactions can also happen when you raise your vibration and activate your higher levels of awareness. In doing so, you increase the disparity between your overall frequency and the lower frequency of the synthetic fragrance. That disparity causes one of the many "ascension symptoms," or physical reactions to expanding consciousness.

Wondering how to find out the safety level of the household products you use? Visit the Resources section at the end of this book for a link to a database that scores thousands of products on their toxicity level.

One of the most insidious forms of toxic fragrance overload can come from using dryer sheets or scented laundry detergent. Consider how much you breathe in the scent from those chemicals while you sleep. Many of the chemicals used in those products are undisclosed carcinogens hiding behind trade secret laws.

While any synthetic product will have a low frequency and a dysregulating effect on the system, there is another option to create beautiful aroma in your home: using essential oils distilled from plants. Like synthetic fragrance, essential oils are still pharmacological (meaning they have a psychological and biological effect on the body), but because they are pure and natural, their power is channeled into raising frequency instead of lowering it.

Unless you're in multiple chemical sensitivity (MCS) crisis mode, most folks can tolerate essential oils and even use them to raise the vibration and clear the energy in your environment.

Organic or wildcrafted rose has the highest measured frequency of any essential oil. Just below that is frankincense and helichrysum. Remember that pesticides sprayed on the plants before harvesting the oil will lower the frequency of an essential oil dramatically, so the purer, the better.

HOW CAN WE THRIVE IN THIS TOXIC WORLD?

It can be easy to bemoan the world we live in, with all of its environmental hazards. But even after my difficult experience with multiple chemical sensitivity, I don't view the world as a dangerous place. More accurately, it's not how I choose to feel in the world. It's my belief that we wouldn't have chosen to incarnate in this era of EMF and chemical pollution if we didn't know, on some level, that we'd be part of the purification of our environment. Older souls don't incarnate to be beaten down. Instead, we come into environments which we know we can purify, elevate, and anchor love into.

The fact is that some people are born with higher frequency than others. The higher the frequency, the more sensitive we are to our environment, as well as foods, incoherent states, sounds, smells, and violence.

As we've talked about, many people with high sensitivity feel that it's a weakness. This engenders an instant judgment around that sensitivity, which then causes them to look for someone or something to blame. Say my neighbor uses dryer sheets, the smell of which flows into my house and causes me to feel terrible. If I'm in a low-vibe state of awareness that positions me as a victim, I might blame my neighbor for being ignorant and using such destructive chemicals, or I could blame my body for not being strong enough to handle dryer sheets.

Judging your body or the things and people around you only reinforces the belief that the earth plane isn't a safe place to incarnate. This leads to a hypervigilant state in which you become so aware that you may start actively looking for emotional injury. This fear-based state only contributes to incoherence, creating a vicious cycle. Fear's only purpose is to create more fear.

The challenge (and where the freedom exists) is to allow yourself to be highly aware while still focusing on maintaining a coherent state. Become aware of your sensitivity without demonizing the factors in your environment that trigger your sensitivity. Then it's much simpler to have access to options to create a physically safer space for yourself. Eventually, you'll be raising your frequency above the frequency of the toxins.

Many times, it's the disparity between your frequency and the low frequency of the toxin that may be creating discomfort or symptoms. However, the more you move into a coherent state, the more you can make conscious choices that improve the situation without anchoring into fear or judgment.

At one point, I remember complaining to my doctor about being so sensitive to chemicals. I was frustrated that other people could wear or be around perfumes without getting a migraine. I was annoyed that others could eat pizza without worrying about MSG. But my doctor explained my state as "Maserati Neurology." Nobody thinks a Maserati is weak if an adjustment needs to be made to a spark plug so the car can function at its optimal level.

Like the Maserati, your high sensitivity is an incredible strength, capable of yielding a beautiful harmonic that the world needs. With that in mind, what better time to honor this sensitivity as a superpower.

WHAT ABOUT THE ENVIRONMENTS YOU CAN'T CHANGE?

To some extent, we can improve our own homes and environments, but we can't control what's in a store, a friend's home, or another public place. There are times when you may choose to be in a place where the environment is undeniably low vibe, like visiting a friend in the hospital or going to a funeral. It could be an environment full of chemical toxins like synthetic fragrance or pesticides, or it could be a room where people have obviously been fighting or crying.

When you've done everything you can do as far as raising the frequency of your body and your environment, there are practices you can do when walking into other people's environments that will maintain your coherence and high vibration, and even help to recalibrate low frequencies.

The most important focus you can have is your intention: tuning into what your conscious intention is and tuning in more deeply to see if there is an unconscious intention. The practice of being in a coherent state that we discussed in Chapter 4 is your most powerful tool. When I walk into a space that's not regulated by the energy protocols I use at home, I tune into the area behind my sternum. I imagine that I'm breathing in and out of my heart center and make a sincere attempt to bring up a restorative emotion, like appreciation, love, or respect. When I do that, I'm affecting the field and intentionally clearing and elevating the space by sending out a coherent wave pattern.

It's about managing and maintaining your own energy, not attempting to dominate or control someone else's energy. There's no guarantee that others in the space will respond to your coherent state by relaxing into a coherent state themselves, even though it's contagious if they consciously *and* unconsciously want to feel better. If someone is still learning from being in an incoherent state, they have every right and responsibility to do that.

When we look at shifting environments through being in a coherent state, we have to remember that everyone has a sovereign choice as to whether or not they also want to make that shift. If they don't want to, there's nothing wrong with that; it's impossible to make a mistake or miss the boat. They are learning valuable lessons and awakening to karmic patterns, or they wouldn't be drawn to that state.

As always, no frequency is bad or good. We can use an environment (just like food) for its intended purpose, which is to help us awaken and move through energies, or move into remembering our true divine nature. Everything will be supportive either indirectly or directly, but it's all Divine Source. If we can remember that, then we won't get scared that low-vibe people, places, or things will contaminate our high frequencies. None of it is to be feared because none of it is bad. It's just about discerning what feels resonant to you.

THE ESSENCE

Your soul chose to be here in this place at this time. Knowing that to be true, there is some type of modulation that can happen in the environment to make sure the pollutants which surround you will not interrupt your spiritual activation. If anything is interrupting your spiritual contribution and your soul's curriculum, something can be done about it. You are innately empowered to elevate all aspects of your life here on earth. That's why this book was written.

An environment which is frequency modulating encourages people to want to make a shift. It works both ways: either we're already creating a shift within us, so we're going to modulate the environment around us, or the environment is modulating to help propel a shift within us.

We can learn how to use the physical body as a tool for expanding consciousness. This begins with taking responsibility for the physical body's wellness and the way it's affected by the environment. For example, if you're aware that EMFs aren't supportive for humans, you'll want to limit your immediate EMF exposure and try an option like FLFE to create harmony. By putting your pineal gland in a position for optimal functioning, you're simultaneously putting yourself in a position for optimal consciousness expansion and awareness. From an optimal position, you're opening up to a natural state. You're moving out of the subnatural into the natural.

CHAPTER 7

———

STEP 3

MEDIA

Throughout my life, anytime I watched TV, what I'd seen would roll around in my brain for hours afterward. This was especially true at night—I'd lie in bed, either awake or in a dream state, my mind running faster and faster. It felt like too much to process. With my level of heightened sensitivity, I was extra open to the information coming at me, and many times, it took all night for my system to process—meaning come back to a centered state again.

When I began to fully understand how conditioning worked, how brainwave states work, I realized this was more than just memories rolling around in my mind. These things were being imprinted in a way that they would become belief systems.

Those belief systems weren't my conscious choice. I couldn't take in this "nourishment" and expect to be full of faith and coherence. I couldn't keep ingesting discordant images and dramatic life-or-death scenarios and expect to feel the way

I want to feel. But like anyone, I had the habit of turning on the TV and using that time to decompress. (Read, "Tune out life so I could just relax," or so I thought.) I needed a reminder of that to fuel my choices so that I wouldn't need to spend so much time detoxifying those unwanted belief systems from my system. My first conscious choice around changing my media diet was putting a cover over my TV with a sign that says, "Contains Programming. Only Watch What You Want to Become."

WATCH WHAT YOU WATCH

That sign still hangs over our TV screen today. It reminds us that there's a reason why shows on TV are known as "programs." When you're watching, reading, listening, you're fully in receiving mode, opening yourself to all that the media contains. Just as with food, the energy we transmit into the world is impacted by the energy within the media we consume.

Within a few minutes of beginning to watch something on TV, your brainwaves typically shift to an alpha state. This is a light hypnotic state—where you are more passive and programmable. The unconscious mind is indiscriminately taking in the messaging that's within whatever program you're watching. By being in this state, watching a screen is equal to programming yourself with whatever is in that show.

Learning this naturally makes people want to be more mindful with what they watch.

However, it's important to know that what's in the program isn't necessarily observable with your eyes or conscious mind. Screens are energetic portals, and as such, they influence our consciousness on an energetic level. As a portal, the screen transmits more than images and story. To truly be discerning about your media consumption, you have to be aware of the conditioning within what you're watching.

I recently saw an old movie from 2007 called *Wild Hogs* with John Travolta. It's about middle-aged men who decide to become bikers and go on an adventurous trip across the country. Partway through the movie, everything is going great for the characters. As he drives down the road on his motorcycle, John Travolta's tightly wound character is having a ton of fun, finally feeling lighthearted and beginning to relax. A moment later, something hits him in the face. It's intended to be a funny moment!

On a conscious level, we may see that moment as comedy and laugh at the unexpected accident. But there's also conditioning beneath what the story is showing us. The message is that as soon as you stop being hypervigilant and begin to let go and be joyful, something unexpected that's bad or painful will happen to you. While the conscious mind is getting a bit of entertainment, the unconscious mind is integrating a reminder to never let its guard down.

This is one small example of a constant in just about all media: the reinforcement of fear programming. Try and think for a moment of media programs that are specifically created with the intention to educate or uplift. Some travel, cooking, and history shows fit the bill. But the vast majority of media, including news programming, is designed to inspire overwhelm, even terror, activating and reinforcing the low-frequency programs embedded in our human DNA.

One that's commonly activated by both the news and by Hollywood is what we could call the doomsday or Armageddon program. This program is all about activating fear, lack of sovereignty, and competition for survival. Think how many doomsday movies populate the big screen each year—from invasion by hostile beings to cataclysmic natural disasters to pandemics to the end of the world.

I'm not saying that all broadcasters are consciously intent on inspiring fear. However, it's understood that fear programming draws people in. Humans are always looking for reinforcement of our frequencies—we unconsciously seek something that validates that we have a right to feel whatever we're feeling. If I generally feel the world is unsafe, I'll go through life unconsciously searching for someone or something to threaten or victimize me, from being cut off in traffic to being denied a promotion to watching crime reports on the news. Even if I'm not an obviously fearful person, and no one can tell my state just by looking at me, it can still be there under the surface, drawing me toward whatever will reinforce my belief that the world isn't safe or fair.

Another deeply embedded program has to do with position relative to others. The ego isn't content with just being—it's always jockeying for position, ranking the "self" as inferior or superior. This is a common motivator for people to watch news or political programs—depending on who is speaking, they'll feel either superior ("That guy is insane!") or inferior ("We're powerless in this situation."). In either case, they are letting their own personal power languish while reinforcing a sense of helplessness and doom.

It all changes when you raise your system's overall frequency to the point where external factors don't destabilize your energy field for any considerable length of time. Through utilizing tools like heart-focused breathing, you can rebalance your field and raise your frequency, regardless of what you're processing through media. It takes some energy but gets easier over time. But until that point, it can be wise to notice how you're affected by media and make a conscious choice to only watch what you want to become. Interestingly, by the time we're able to easily shift media energies in our systems, we typically have lost our appetite for the low-vibe stuff anyway!

Just like with the food we put in our bodies, the clothing we put on our bodies, or the cars we drive, we want to think deeply and feel into the media we consume. Not only the content of it but the energy in which it was created, since that energy informs the frequency that is then transmitted to us. Just as you may choose locally grown organic food over factory-farmed conventional food if it's accessible to you, the way media is produced has an impact on your overall health by the frequency it requires you to process. Whatever media we consume holds the frequency of all the different people involved, as well as the frequency of their workplace in creating that media.

This is why you can watch a great movie but be exhausted afterward. You're likely processing many different experiences, locations, and belief systems that were transmitted through that movie, some of which may be noticeable within the film's story or production and some which are invisible physically but super impactful energetically.

Thinking of TV or other media as just entertainment, a pleasant distraction that everyone engages in, is a way of giving up your self-authority. Just because it's culturally acceptable and popular doesn't change its impact on your energy. If you feel uncomfortable about some of the media that you consume but continue to invest energy in it, that becomes a double whammy inner conflict: the impact of the actual programming, plus the unconscious choice to give up your self-authority.

MAKING FRIENDS WITH YOUR AMYGDALA

As we've talked about previously, the amygdala sets the overall tone for your entire emotional system. It begins to crave whatever you consistently receive, as well as single experiences that significantly affect you. Over time, you'll start seeking things that give you the same experience over and over.

This might sound like you're at the mercy of your amygdala, but it's actually good news. Yes, that mechanism helps program your amygdala with fearful low-frequency beliefs and judgments, but you can also recondition it to support heart-brain coherence.

The first approach is to start making conscious choices with the media you consume. If you start reprogramming the amygdala with a diet of high-frequency media consumption, you'll train it to release the hormone of relaxation and awareness around high-frequency things. Over time, you'll have less and less desire for low-frequency media—it won't help you relax or unwind anymore. You'll also begin sending out a signal for other experiences that bring you a feeling of relaxation and awareness.

Another technique is to promote heart-brain coherence in other parts of your life. Meditating on appreciation is the key to this in my life. The more time I spend contemplating in gratitude for the things, people, and environment in my life, the more I program my brain to experience gratitude anywhere I happen to be. This, again, sends out a signal that brings people and events into my life that will fill me with appreciation and promote an integrated, coherent, balanced, aware, relaxed state.

The relationship between relaxed and aware is important. The ideal state of being is a relaxed state of awareness, which allows for a high level of functionality along with a centered, calm body.

A media fast can be highly supportive. It doesn't have to be too dramatic—just a week without turning on the TV or shutting down your phone or computer after 7:00 p.m. can start the cleansing process. The length of this fast will be different for everyone, depending on their frequency and how they process media. You'll know how much it's been impacting you, by how much you crave it when you shut it off for a few days. Personally, while I tend to process energy upgrades very quickly, at times I'm a slow processor when it comes to media due to heightened sensitivity. For this reason, I have abstained from watching anything violent or emotionally intense for many years. I'm making a conscious choice to conserve energy and use my sleep time for healing rather than processing undigested media. That may not be the best choice for everyone, but this is about learning what works best for you.

If you've been watching TV or using the internet before bed, it can be very helpful to add a practice of a sleep declaration right before bed. Choose an intentional statement that is uplifting and will set the stage for your energy as you sleep. You can either say it out loud or write it down and look at it before going to sleep—either way, it makes a huge difference.

Here's one that I like: "I now dedicate my sleep time to my healing and to my spiritual expansion. I commit to knowing myself beyond the limitations of fear and allow my sleep to support that mission."

The goal isn't to negate media consumption from your life completely unless that feels supportive and sustainable for you. The overall goal could be to stabilize your energy to the point where you can potentially watch anything and it won't destabilize you, because your coherent state is able to transmute those energies. Once you reach that milestone, you'll probably notice your tastes have changed, and you don't even crave low-vibe media anymore. In the meantime, supporting your physical, emotional, spiritual, and energetic bodies through conscious choice paves the way.

CHAPTER 8

STEP 4

RELATIONSHIPS

The topic of relationships is such a deep and complex topic that I actually teach an entire course on it. While I can't delve into every aspect in this book, relationships are such a major influence in our lives that I wanted to address it.

As we awaken and raise frequency, it's normal to have phases where our current patterns feel stuck, and relationships are a big part of this.

The low-frequency response to this opportunity is to repeat a story about the other person or yourself, or to adopt a new culturally prominent one. For the past few years, there's been a growing trend in which people refer to a relationship (or the other person in it) as toxic.

While I understand how that term is meant to help people recognize when a relationship is unhealthy, it can be misleading. Labeling itself can be what's toxic, in that it creates a duality mindset that can impact a person's overall frequency.

We talked in earlier chapters about how situations aren't stressful in themselves; the stress comes from our perception. In the same way, a relationship, a person, or even a behavior are not inherently toxic. A person can't make you feel a certain way, much less act in a certain way. Pointing outside yourself to the source of toxicity takes away your responsibility for your experience, mindset, and frequency.

The way you perceive and process the relationship based on your conditioning, mindset, and frequency are what causes the stress in it. Every relationship is a living consciousness field. Just as the unified field includes the input of all living beings, the relationship field is always responding to what energies you and your partner (or friend, child, boss, parent) are putting in and taking out.

When we are in a relationship, it's tempting to adopt different cultural and social trends for expression and look for the ways another being fulfills these definitions of behavior. But that habit tends to reinforce a lack of self-authority and self-responsibility—instead of choosing how you want to feel, you're letting cultural trends define your experience. This tendency interferes with the process of activating your natural intuitive nature. Moreover, it can prevent you from understanding the deepest-level *why* behind your experience. As long as you perceive yourself or others as being inherently a certain type of person (toxic, needy, abusive, damaged, etc.), you're also perceiving yourself as a certain type of person: disempowered, victimized, unlucky. The pattern of blaming another for how we feel implies that we have handed over our authority and power to that person.

But here's the thing to remember: giving your power to

another being will not do them any good. It's not theirs to use, and it's impossible for them (or you) to benefit from that misplaced, unqualified power.

If we're not willing to examine ourselves and discontinue blaming others, nothing will change. If you say, "This person is just like that," you'll stay in that loop. It's not a great feeling. If we're in a situation that is abusive in any way, we must remember that because of the way the brain/hormone axis works, it can be very difficult to acknowledge the toll it's taking and actually take action on our own behalf. The conditioning/tendency to sacrifice our own well-being to keep the peace is what must shift, not the other person. And reaching out for support many times is the only way to break out of the loop.

The same thing is true when you examine your own tendencies around relationships. Saying to yourself, "I always go after this type," or "My dad was always angry, and that's why I'm drawn to men with anger issues," just reinforces the idea that you're powerless.

Raising frequency requires owning your role in every perception, including that of a relationship. A good place to start is with the amygdala and its tendency to get addicted to its previous experience. If I grew up in a stressful home full of fighting and needless drama, even if I didn't consciously like it, I might be addicted to that drama and stress. This would lead me to unconsciously seek out relationships that give me that feeling. The only way to interrupt that pattern is to make a conscious choice to create something else.

If you find yourself in that stuck place, where the old pattern doesn't align with what you want to experience anymore, consider it a golden opportunity to raise frequency. Stop telling yourself the same old story, and ask yourself questions that raise your conditioning to the surface.

- "What is it that I'm experiencing?"
- "When is the first time I've ever experienced it?"
- "What is it in me that wants to reinforce whatever this belief is?"
- "For me to have this relationship or be attracted to this type of person, what must I believe about myself and about life?"

SPIRITUAL PARTNERSHIP

As your awakening progresses, it's natural to want others to join you in your growing state of coherence.

The energy we take in and release in our relationships can change. Let's say you have a group of friends where the friendships are generally focused on something that, as you awaken, begins to feel out of alignment—perhaps it's based around gossip, complaining, low-vibe media, or putting yourselves or others down. When the shift happens within us, the typical first stage is to move into judgment. You might move into superiority ("I can't take how superficial those people are."), or you might move into an inferior role ("Why can't I just relax around these people? What's wrong with me?").

Know that when you move through your awakening process, it's normal to have people in your life fall away or feel that you're not as connected with the people you once connected with. That frequency differential between people can sometimes lead you to feel alone, like no one understands you.

This is particularly painful when it happens within a couple. They may have always watched the nightly news together, but then one of them is in an awakening phase and, along with that, has a heightening of their sensitivity to media (as we talked about in the last chapter). This shift can be jarring, leaving both to wonder why they can't enjoy things together anymore.

If this isolation, and the judgment that typically accompanies it, is allowed to grow, it can create a real divide in the relationship. People might come to feel like they can't even be in the same room with someone when they're engaged in something both used to enjoy. It can be challenging to not try to tell people what they need to do—"I can't handle this. You need to turn it off." Older souls, however, might be more apt to suffer through it and say nothing for fear of rocking the boat until they just can't anymore. Either way builds resentment within a relationship.

If you're in this situation, it might feel as though you're being forced to choose between your awakening and the relationship. But I promise that isn't the case. Even if other people don't understand, you can still make the changes you're feeling led to make. As you embody more and more of your highest self, your energy stabilizes to where you can say what feels true for you without putting judgment into the field. In that scenario, you can have ease while living with someone who wants to do what no longer feels supportive for you. Being in a harmonious relationship isn't about controlling someone else's behavior—it's about taking the best care of yourself right now and allowing the other to do what feels true for them.

Eventually, there's a live-and-let-live energy that emerges with this feeling: "If this no longer feels supportive, I don't feel a reason to do it. But I don't have to make the other person wrong to justify me making shifts in my life."

This can be a lot harder when you're in an enmeshed or codependent relationship, which many people mistake as being deeply romantic and close. Few people have a good picture of a non-codependent relationship because we don't see it exemplified as much in depictions of a healthy partnership.

BECOMING YOUR OWN SPIRITUAL PARTNER

When you're in the midst of conscious awakening, the most powerful thing you can do for any relationship you're in is to learn to be a spiritual partner to yourself first. This doesn't constitute abandoning your partner. Rather, it's taking the opportunity to set a new inner pattern in place that will ultimately raise the frequency of your relationship.

When you're a spiritual partner to yourself, you learn to observe yourself without bias or judgment. You can tune into your own patterns and conditioning while, at the same time, nourishing yourself with unconditional love. The more you do this, the more you're able to see and appreciate the divinity within yourself and develop awareness of your own sovereignty and mission on this earth.

As this loving awareness grows within you, it naturally overflows to other people in your life. Without trying, you can notice how your partner is exploring their human experience—not from a place of impatience or criticism, but from a high-frequency place of love and honor for their individual

choices, remembering that they have their own soul's curriculum that's driving their behavior.

Being able to observe someone else in this way shifts everything about how you relate to them. It begets an expression
of emotion from your deepest heart center. When you're
not being a spiritual partner to yourself, there's a tendency
to hide this expression because it may feel too vulnerable.
But feeling the encompassing love and support of your own
personal inner spiritual partnership creates safety within
so that you can open your heart to anyone and everyone.
You know there might be pain along the way, but you don't
fear it. If your partner hurts you, you can still love them
and appreciate the journey, while choosing not to be in that
person's space.

This is key in deciding whether to exit a relationship. Rather
than running from it out of fear, anger, blame, or disillusion-
ment, you can see from a higher-level perspective what will be
most supportive for you and choose what to do from a place
of loving wisdom. Remember that what's supportive and right
for you (in your highest good) is *always* supportive for others
and in their highest good, even if that's not obvious just yet.
There are no exceptions to this universal law. (Of course, there
are different considerations if one is in an abusive relationship.
In those cases, move quickly to safety and process what you've
learned afterward.) Rather than blaming the other person for
the end of the relationship, you can move forward in your
life with a high-frequency lens of compassion on that person,
releasing them to their blessings as you accept yours. My book
How Old Is Your Soul? covers relationship differentials based
on soul age and may be helpful for further exploration.

Spiritual self-love releases the potential for judgment of yourself for how you feel, as well as the fear of judgment from your partner. It also brings incredible freedom. Rather than feeling like you have to show up as the person your partner expects you to be, you can be exactly who you are, knowing that is who your partner's highest self truly wants you to be. (Even if that means expressing anger or frustration. Authenticity becomes paramount over keeping the peace.) Rather than feeling like you have to control your partner with how you express love, you can choose to radiate it with reckless abandon, the way a child runs into the arms of their parents.

Whether they choose to receive it is up to them. But you've released any worry of being judged for who you are, how you feel, or for your expression of it. You're living directly from your truth, your heart.

LEARNING TO BE A SPIRITUAL PARTNER

Being a spiritual partner to yourself means that your first priority is taking responsibility for your own feelings, clearing your own emotional landscape, and supporting your own spiritual life first. But once you feel so supported by having done it for yourself, you have plenty of energy available to support someone else in their spiritual life.

Taking responsibility for your own support necessitates a large amount of self-care and self-love. The reason I can be a great spiritual partner to Zack, to my son, and to my parents is because I take really good care of myself. When I put my restorative time on the back burner, I'm less connected because I'm running on fumes.

For many old souls, the most renewal we get comes from solitude. Old souls in particular enjoy spending time alone, even if it's just an hour of having the house to yourself, being outside alone, or just sitting. It's incredible how restorative that is for many old souls. Not all, but many old souls tend to feel more drained by being with people and more restored by being alone.

I'm definitely restored by time alone, and so many times, I'll get up an hour or sometimes even two hours earlier than anyone else in the house, including the dogs, because I want to have that time alone. Sometimes, I'll sit outside when the sun isn't even out yet. Maybe I'll meditate or write or read or just contemplate. Doesn't matter what I'm doing, I'm focused on being. That way, when the animals and people are in need of my attention, I have it to give.

YOUR PART IN BALANCING ENERGY

When you have a deep emotional history with someone, it can be hard to discern how much of what you're processing comes from you and how much comes from you trying to process for the other person. It's common for people in a close relationship to match each other's energy, either directly or indirectly. Depending on the situation and our own state at the time, we might heighten our energy when someone else's energy heightens or do the adverse and lower our energy. If a furious person walks into a room, you might be more likely to speak quietly and make yourself very calm, trying to use your energy field to calm that person down. But if their fury is directed at you, you might try to dominate and yell back. This is all normal when we bear unresolved wounds, thanks to universal spiritual laws like reciprocity and projection.

In addition, most older souls have empathic tendencies, which essentially means feeling other people's feelings. However, this often leads to processing discordant energies for other people all the time. In a relationship, we often don't even realize we're doing it. If your partner is having a challenging time at work, you might feel yourself more tired, stressed, or overwhelmed.

This also may come from how you kept the peace in your childhood home. Maybe you grew up always feeling responsible for your parents or feeling that you were the one holding the energy in the home stable, so you may have an ingrained conditioning to try to keep energy stable by using your own energy or emotional body.

Again, processing another person's energy is perfectly normal and natural, and it can be helpful when it's done consciously. This is what many lightworkers do—we use our own field to channel high-vibrational energy that provides healing for another. But when it's done reflexively, without conscious awareness, it's not very helpful, and there isn't a reason for it.

After collective trauma incidents have occurred, such as mass shootings, police violence, or the 2020 pandemic, I've heard so many people in our Raw Spirituality Community ask, "Why am I so tired? I'm exhausted." There are many people who feel like they can't get off the couch after a trauma or intense time in our culture. This is because they are processing the shock, grief, and trauma in the collective. Extreme self-care is the antidote.

As a lightworker, you likely have that natural "I'm of service" energy within you. But to do the most good, it's important to find the most efficient use of that energy. When a partner saying, "I feel terrible" makes you feel equally terrible, it leads to a push-pull of who feels worse, who's going to take care of the other one or who's not going to get their needs met. It creates a situation in which each individual's own energy works against them as you both simultaneously comfort and compete with each other in an effort to stay close.

Furthermore, it ends up having the opposite effect from what you intend. Taking on and processing your partner's feelings robs them of their opportunity to process what their soul is guiding them to learn and gather wisdom from and through.

My son is an adult, and the mom part of me (my human) at times still wants to go to his house and do his laundry and solve whatever issues come up so that he can just enjoy his life freely. But the part of me that has grown wiser doesn't do that. Upgraded service is born of activated wisdom through consciousness.

In the same way, we can take care of a sick family member without worrying, feeling overwhelmed, or lowering our immune system. We can compassionately sit with someone who's suffering and not process all their suffering through our emotional and physical bodies.

Fortunately, there are plenty of ways to support others' energy without processing it through your own system.

ACKNOWLEDGE THE IMPACT

It's important to remember that when one person in a relationship shifts, the whole dynamic shifts. As we've seen in other aspects of diet, expansion can create instability at first.

It's temporary, but it can be so destabilizing that some people aren't able to maintain relationships through it, especially if the relationship was based on one or both partners sacrificing themselves.

If you have two people living in a house who are both heavy drinkers, who drink every single day, and one person stops, that affects everything. It affects how you've been connecting and what you expect from each other. It affects how you wake up together and how you spend your evenings.

This is just as true for raising frequency. Even if nothing else about you has changed, this shift changes everything, for you and for your partner. Just as you are wired for familiarity, so is your partner. Even if what you're putting into the unified field is objectively better (trust over anxiety, authenticity over repression, etc.), the unfamiliarity of this new consciousness can be a trigger/catalyst for low-frequency emotions (fear, confusion, judgment) in your partner. Many times a partner can feel abandoned when you're no longer in the same frequency range with them.

It can help a lot in this situation to let your partner know that you're making a shift. Often, explaining that shift in detail only creates more confusion, so it's fine to simply say, "There are some things about the way I view the world and myself that are changing. Just please bear with me as I grow through this."

There have been a few times over the course of my son's life when I would say to him, "Normally, I would answer you with this kind of response, but now, I won't because I'm shifting. I realize that might be new and different for you." This happened most when he was a teenager and sometimes caused some normal teen reactions from him. To his credit, he'd come back and say, "I'm just used to you being a certain way, and now you're not anymore, and I need to get used to it."

I find getting everything out on the table is far better than quietly hoping that whoever you live with will go back to being who they were before. Talking about it can be a really powerful catalyst for change in your partner, as well. However, for some personality types there's no way to help them see a shift as a positive thing. For example, someone with abandonment issues may hear you saying, "I want to change myself," and hear it as a threat that you might possibly leave them. It's also possible that your partner will take you changing as a personal judgment against them, assuming that you expect them to change along with you.

You can't control your partner's reaction to your awakening, nor would we want to, so know your audience even as you do your best to be as transparent as possible. It's not something you can hide—the information and the transformation will be in the field, and they will pick up on it on one or more levels.

LEAD WITH LOVE

When you're raising the frequency of your relationship, conventional thinking says that it's all about separation—these are your problems to work on, and these are mine. But as you start upgrading your relationship to a higher frequency, you recognize that it's all about unification. Everything that another person goes through is a human experience, and as such, you can relate to it even if you've never had that same experience in your life. When both partners focus on unity within oneself, it dissolves the barriers while creating bridges between each partner's higher self.

This doesn't require both partners being engaged in the same way with raising frequency. You or your partner may sometimes attempt to connect within low-frequency energy in moments of triggering or survival-based emotions. In those moments, rather than isolating or abandoning the other, you can honor their choice while continuing to move up into coherence. The more you choose that experience, the more you can meet there to share your experience without one person being a rescuer and one person needing to be rescued.

RECOGNIZE TRIGGERS

Another popular cultural pattern is to avoid triggers at all costs—causing them as well as experiencing them. Conventional thinking advises that you keep anyone who triggers you at a distance, or tiptoeing around the one whom you tend to trigger.

A higher consciousness recognizes triggers for what they are: a most powerful catalyst accompanied by the sensation of an old wound getting laid bare. While it may set off a cascade of low-frequency emotions, recognizing this as an exciting opportunity for healing will help you shift into a higher frequency response to those emotions and use the trigger/catalyst as it's meant to be used.

Shifting your response to being triggered yourself will help you do the same for your partner when they are triggered. Being partners in life often means being partners in healing, and when one person gets triggered by something, their reaction can potentially trigger the other. In that moment, one partner has to choose to put their trigger on the back burner for just a minute and serve the other as a healing partner. Doing this requires trusting that you'll get what you need at some point and being brave enough to help the other person through their triggers in this moment before dealing with your own. Doing this is incredibly powerful to upgrade the frequency of your relationship.

We have some great tools for exploring this in our Spiritual Partnership online course. It's designed for those who are not currently in a partnership and those who are, as well as those "it's complicated" relationships.

LOVING VALIDATION

Spiritual partnership allows you to compassionately acknowledge your partner's emotion without processing it through your own system. As you raise frequency, you learn to validate someone else, understanding that validation is not agreement. Validation is affirming other people's right to feel whatever they feel and to process that feeling in whatever way feels appropriate for them. In doing this, you're not judging them or giving them permission, but instead affirming their sovereignty.

When you honor someone's experience without taking it over or coloring it with your own energy, it creates an intimacy utterly unlike anything you may have experienced before.

Most people feel close as a result of shared worry or trauma, but bonding through honoring each other's sovereignty creates closeness that is uniquely transformative.

As long as we see ourselves as separate from our highest self, we also feel separate from each other. But once I can acknowledge both your sovereignty and my own, I can allow for the natural connectedness that we all have without crossing over into codependency. It might seem like a really fine line, but with practice, it becomes second nature, and then finally, first nature.

MAKING NEW DECISIONS

Sometimes, the differential between your state of awakening and your partner's can lead to a point of decision about whether to stay in the relationship or not. While this can be a relatively easy decision within a short-term relationship of a few weeks or even months, it's a real conundrum for people who have been partnered for a long time, especially if you have a family together.

If you choose to consider this decision, know that any choice you make is okay. It's not about staying or going—it's about the energy behind your choice and the speed of it.

If I decide to break up with someone because I believe he is entirely culpable for our problems, I'm not really ending the relationship. I'm only reinforcing a pattern that will follow me into the next partnership. The only way to break that pattern is to make decisions based on love.

This doesn't mean letting someone walk all over you or trying to rescue the other person or remaining in a relationship that doesn't support you (which means it's also not supporting them). It's about finding the best way to create an environment that feels supportive to the overall energy of love. If the best way to do that is without that person in your life, that is okay. It's also okay to keep loving someone who is acting hurtfully toward you or themselves. The most important thing is to understand what the energy of coherent love feels like. As you support yourself with that love, you'll naturally know what the most appropriate choice is for you—whether to be with someone on a daily basis or no longer be connected with them.

As long as you are in the relationship, there are adjustments you can make that allow you to remain in that relationship in a way that feels more aligned with your higher self. A big one is letting go of resentment by speaking up from a loving place about what doesn't feel good to you. It can mean creating an energetic buffer that lets you restore your coherent state between interactions.

Say you have a friend who does nothing but complain every time they call. You could create a buffer of time. Instead of having a boundary where you think, "Ugh, I just can't talk to this person," you could consider, "I can't talk to them all the time, but what really feels great is if I talk with them every other week. If I talk to them every other day, I don't feel so great."

Being in a spiritual partnership with someone requires living from your heart center with them. If you're not able to support that in your current state of partnership, that might be a reason to create more distance between you. Honor what it is that you need while knowing that need isn't because of someone else or what they are or aren't doing.

If I believe that I love someone as long as they do what I want them to do and act the way I want them to act, that isn't actually love. It's familiarity coupled with control.

THE RESCUER CYCLE

For some people, there can be an inclination to stay in a relationship so that you can "fix" the other person with your higher consciousness. Where there's real love, it can be tempting to believe that your own growth will provoke the other person to desire growth as well. That certainly can happen, but it depends more on the other person's willingness and their karmic curriculum, rather than on the role you play in their life.

It's important to acknowledge that not everyone is willing to expand their spiritual consciousness, and many will even resist their own awakening process. They might dig their heels into their own evolution, clinging to their stories about how they've been mistreated or victimized. We can't pressure people into having awareness. It's beautiful when it happens, but it won't always happen in our current incarnation.

If you're choosing to stay in a relationship, give yourself loving permission to authentically experience your own journey. As humans, there can be a tendency to expect some external standard of perfection within what's meant to be a learning process. We have two choices: to tear ourselves down for our perceived mistakes or to see the catalyst in every choice.

If a part in your mind worries about what could have led you to act out of a lower frequency, look deeply into the core of what you did and acknowledge that it was the very best you had in a given moment. Once we recognize everything is part of an overall learning process, we'll see that all of our life events either directly or indirectly supported our expansion and evolution.

MIRROR ENERGY

There are ancient stories in some cultures about how every being in life is a mirror—the way you perceive your partner reflects aspects of yourself and vice versa. This happens because of the interconnectedness of all living things. We're all cells in the body of the Divine Source, which gives us an ability to reflect each other's thoughts and emotions back to each other, often without even knowing that we're doing it. Nothing goes unsaid in the energy world. Whatever frequencies exist in the heart and the head are flowing into the field.

This creates a beautiful closeness between spiritual partners. But it also serves a beautiful purpose in a relationship that may seem toxic.

Many years ago, I was in a relationship with someone who frequently criticized and yelled at me. I spent a lot of time trying to figure out how I was attracting this energy from him since I wasn't verbally critical toward him. Eventually, I realized he was mirroring the energy of my own inner voice. Even though I didn't yell at him or criticize him, I was sending my own hypercritical self-talk into the field, and he was expressing it out loud.

Strange as it might sound, I have enormous gratitude for his role in my life. Despite the pain I felt at the time, this person was enormously supportive in an indirect way. He brought contrast into my life that was a powerful learning tool, allowing me to see something about how I viewed myself that I couldn't see before, and I honor him and our past relationship for that. I chose to leave the relationship behind, but seeing him through this lens of gratitude made it easier to forgive him, as well as myself, for the suffering that had taken place during that time. He was a teacher who helped illuminate what I wasn't previously able to address.

No matter what your relationship status might be today, you have the opportunity to learn from contrast every day if you're willing to perceive it. Any treatment you don't like is a form of indirect support in your expansion process. It's just a matter of being awake enough and willing to learn from it rather than defensive of the decisions that brought you there.

If you feel ignored or victimized or pushed into a rescuer role by someone, that person is serving you as a teacher, revealing a higher level of truth. You might not be able to see it yet, but know higher truths are available to you whenever you're ready. It's impossible to force awakening. It's okay not to know what you don't know. You will likely have an awareness about it in a week, a day, or a year that you don't have right now. Again, there are no mistakes in our natural expansion process. As you reach new vantage points along your journey, the knowledge you need will become clear to you. It always does.

"TO BE COMPLETE, YOU NEED PARTNERSHIP"

After all this discussion about the relationship element of your diet, you may have concluded that having a relationship is a necessary part of raising your spiritual consciousness. Given our culture's not-so-subtle assumption that people (especially females) need a partnership to be complete, this idea might be incredibly frustrating. So let me say clearly that no one needs a partner, not even a spiritual partner, in order to raise their frequency and upgrade their consciousness. *Having a physical partner in the physical world has no bearing on how complete we are as beings.* We are made whole and complete, and we recognize/remember this more and more as we move into unity within ourselves.

If you choose to have a relationship in physical form, that's great. But instead of having this "you complete me" mind-set, the mindset can be, "I am complete and open to having a relationship with another being who is also discovering completion within him or herself." This interdependence protects you from falling into a victim or rescuer role, as well as from moving into a place of judgment toward yourself, your partner, or the relationship.

Noticing judgment is also very important for those who want a relationship but haven't found one yet. Know that you aren't on the wrong track if you haven't found the partner you desire—you wouldn't have this desire if it weren't part of your karmic curriculum. Not having found a spiritual partner yet doesn't mean that there's something wrong with you, and there's no "missing piece" that will instantly cause your soul mate to show up. It merely means that your soul has given you more time to elevate into a higher frequency, and so has your potential partner's soul. Keep doing your work so that when you come together, your union will be that much sweeter and more satisfying.

THE ESSENCE

Have you ever considered the concept of there being three beings in every relationship, each of the two people and then the relationship itself as a third entity. In many writings over the years, a tree is given as a symbol for the relationship: giving shade, providing food, and something to lean on. It's a great metaphor in that it illustrates how the relationship itself is a living consciousness field: it receives and transmits energy just as you and your partner do, based on the ways each partner contributes from their individual consciousness field.

What is the most important aspect of spiritual partnership? Becoming a spiritual partner to ourselves: a gentle, kind, loving energy behind our self-understanding, inner voice, and self-talk. When we become spiritual partners to ourselves, we actually marry the higher self with the lower self. The unification of your own mind, body, soul, and spirit is the primary relationship. As you expand individually through spiritual partnership of yourself, you'll radiate compassion and love into the field, creating a coherent state that attracts all sorts of spiritual partners—some romantic and some platonic, some that last a lifetime and some that are sweetly fleeting. All are heart-expanding catalysts for our spiritual journey.

CHAPTER 9

———

YOUR STEP-BY-STEP PLAN

It's time to bring all the elements of the Third Eye Diet together. As I mentioned way back in Chapter 1, sometimes it can feel destabilizing to make a sudden, total shift from low-frequency consumption to high frequency. For that reason, I suggest taking it easy on yourself with a gradual shift in all aspects of your diet.

It's also important to make it as rewarding as possible. I don't advocate for quitting a habit cold turkey unless that feels true and sustainable for you. Instead, try this: whatever you choose to remove from your diet can be replaced with at least one, preferably two, new things that are fun, interesting, or pleasurable. You'll go a lot farther if you really feel the difference between the old energy that was challenging for you and the new energy that is supportive for you. It's time to get excited—this is self-love in action!

STEP ONE: MEDITATION

Meditation is the first and most important step in raising frequency and awakening your intuitive senses. Your energetic blueprint (i.e., the physical/mental/emotional/energetic state you're cultivating) when you first begin your day determines whether or not you'll stay in the same energy flow as yesterday or move into conscious creation.

Whenever I talk to students about meditation, I make a point of defusing the overwhelm that so many people feel around this idea. All that meditation really means is choosing a specific single focus that has the energy blueprint (which includes the emotion) you're choosing to integrate. If we want today to be an upgrade from yesterday, we have to make a conscious choice to create the energy we'll ride for the day. As the old saying goes, nothing changes until you do.

I strongly recommend meditating every day at least once a day. Ideally, it would be the first thing you do upon getting up in the morning and the last thing you do before bed. By doing this, you'll consciously set an energetic blueprint for your day.

When you wake up, you're in an alpha state, the ideal place to be for meditation. That's why it's important to meditate before you look at anything else that will change your brainwave state into beta or high beta (a state of either learning or stress).

You can start by listening to a guided meditation or some chanting if you like. You could also begin by moving into coherence and building those grateful feelings. Let the feelings build and start to feel your vibration raise in relation to the emotions that you're consciously generating. Finish by getting excited about how amazing it feels to take charge of your own energy and how this is setting the tone for your entire day.

> The word "meditation" can encompass a lot, so I specifically recommend coherence meditation. We have lots of meditations in our Raw Spirituality Community at RawSpirituality.com. Two great places to start are the "Coherence Mastery Guided Meditation," along with the "Raise Your Frequency Meditation."

TIPS FOR OPTIMAL MEDITATION

I know it's tempting, but avoid meditating while lying down. Lying down is relaxation, not meditation. When you meditate sitting up, you allow the energy in the central channel along the spine to flow vertically up into the higher centers and down into the earth plane, and this helps in a whole lot of ways.

Close your eyelids and gently roll your eyes up toward the center of your brow. You may feel slight pressure as your third eye chakra begins to activate. (If it feels uncomfortable, lower your chin slightly.) This action supports an alpha brainwave state, which assists in meditation, but it also puts you in a very light hypnotic, programmable state.

For this reason, don't meditate while listening to anything that would be considered negative or that has a low vibration.

I support my meditation with subtle energy products, such as mandalas, images, and MP3s that broadcast supportive energetic signatures. (You can scan the QR code here with your phone camera or go to

AlyssaMalehorn.com/faves to find the products I find most supportive and helpful.) These can be digitally accessed—just open up an image or MP3 on your phone, and it immediately starts broadcasting energy.

Eventually, we arrive at a level of consciousness where all of life becomes a meditation. In this state, you observe your experiences and yourself from a loving, compassionate witness perspective, without being drawn into the illusion of duality (good/bad/right/wrong). One of the ways to reach that point is through a regular meditation practice. You'll know when you've gotten to that point when your days feel balanced and your state observable, even when you didn't take the time to meditate. You experience the peaceful awareness that comes from meditation all day long, no matter what you're doing.

One of my favorite MP3s influences your brain to produce alpha, beta, theta, gamma, and delta brainwaves all in perfect proportion to each other, like someone would after years of meditating. See my website AlyssaMalehorn.com/faves for the "Awaken the Mind" link.

STEP TWO: PRACTICE COHERENCE THROUGHOUT THE DAY

Practice coherence throughout the day by consciously cultivating feelings of gratitude. A great place to do this regularly is while driving since you're in a semihypnotic state with your eyes trained forward on the road. Focus your awareness on your heart center and bring up thoughts and feelings of deep gratitude. It can be for something you're listening to, for getting to share that drive time with family, for the beautiful trees, or even for being able to just sit there and be if you're stuck in traffic.

You can do this same exercise anywhere you happen to be—eating lunch in a meeting, going for a run, having a conversation with another parent in the school pickup line, playing with your pet, even watching TV. Focusing your awareness on your heart center and breathing in and out of the heart, while considering what you're grateful for, is the most powerful practice you can incorporate into daily life.

The key is just practicing being in this coherent energy of love as often as possible, in as many different settings and situations as possible. You're building up that muscle so that when you're under pressure, moving into coherence is natural and easy instead of seemingly unreachable.

STEP THREE: BLESS YOUR FOOD

Moving into a coherent state before you eat is a powerful way to broadcast gratitude and love, especially with your food and drink positioned directly in front of your heart center.

Here are some of my favorite blessings that help raise my frequency around meals:

- I am so grateful for this clean food and water, for the opportunity to be here on this planet at this time, to be in service and love. I am filled with gratitude for all that is the source of infinite love. Thank you, thank you, thank you, and so it is.
- This food is a gift, a collaboration of the earth, sun, sky, and water. I give thanks to all elements and energies in contribution to my physical and spiritual well-being. Thank you.

- May all be fed. May all be healed. May all be loved.[4]
- May this food restore our strength, giving new energy to our limbs, new thoughts to our minds.
- May this drink restore our souls, giving new vision to our spirits, new warmth to our hearts.[5]

STEP FOUR: CHOOSE ONE LOW-VIBE FOOD TO REPLACE WITH TWO HIGH-VIBE FOODS

In my experience, the easiest way to shift your patterns around food and drink is to replace one low-vibe food with two high-vibe options. For example, if you're ready to let go of the low-vibe energy around eating red meat, you might add in a replacement like bananas and coconut butter. If you want to replace artificial sweeteners, you could add dates and maple syrup for sweetness in your life.

STEP FIVE: CHOOSE ONE LOW-VIBE DRINK TO REPLACE WITH TWO HIGH-VIBE DRINKS

The principle is the same as with food. If you feel that your energy isn't supported by drinking wine every night, you can replace it with a nourishing evening drink like golden milk or a soothing herbal tea, and add in a high-vibe smoothie in the mornings. Now, instead of spending all day waiting for one special treat, you get to enjoy a delicious treat twice a day while also raising your frequency.

We've included my favorite recipe for Golden Milk in the Resources section at the end of this book. For those who

---

4 John Robbins, co-founder of Food Revolution Network, www.JohnRobbins.info, *May All Be Fed.*

5 Source unknown.

don't want to make it from scratch, Gaia Herbs also has a premade golden milk powder that you can simply add to any plant milk of your choice.

STEP SIX: CHOOSE ONE LOW-VIBE MEDIA OUTLET AND REPLACE IT WITH ONE MEDIA OUTLET THAT LIFTS YOU UP, *PLUS* AN UPLIFTING ACTION

Think about how you spend your time before bed. Do you go to sleep feeling a low-vibe sense of relief that your stresses are over (for now) or eager to recover from the mental or emotional triggers that have bothered you throughout the day? If so, considering your media consumption can be a helpful way to raise your frequency while sleeping and get better sleep in the process.

Are there forms of media that make you feel like you lose yourself? Are there forms that you have to emotionally or mentally recover from after you've consumed them? Or perhaps you emotionally numb yourself during and afterward to try to remain balanced? Whatever comes to mind, replace one of them with a form of media that lifts you up, and pair it with an uplifting action.

For example, maybe you spend the last hour before bed scrolling through Instagram. You may not really mean to spend that much time, but it's easy to get lost in it, and before you know it, an hour has gone by. Instead of doing that, try reading a few pages of an uplifting book or listening to guided meditation. Then take action, such as writing about your worries in a journal, followed by what you're grateful for from that day.

STEP SEVEN: REPLACE ONE TOXIC PRODUCT IN YOUR HOME WITH TWO NONTOXIC PRODUCTS

Tune up your environment by replacing low-vibe products with high-vibe alternatives. This tends to be pretty easy for most people, so challenge yourself to choose alternatives that benefit more than just you. For example, the synthetic fragrance oils used in most scented candles not only make your body work harder (as we talked about in Chapter 6), but they also tend to be made by companies that pollute our rivers, lakes, oceans, and air. By replacing one of those scented candles with two natural candles, you're supporting the planet's health as well as your own.

Both in our home and in our office, we infuse the space with natural candles made by the women of a nonprofit in Nashville, Tennessee, who are recovering from trafficking, abuse, and addictions. Not only do they raise the frequency of the space through a natural, essential-oil fragrance, but they also raise our collective frequency by supporting our fellow humans. I offer these candles in my shop at AlyssaMalehorn.com.

It's true that you might pay a little more for natural, non-toxic, ethically created cleaning products. Before reflexively objecting to it, recognize what those expenses really mean. Is your overall health worth an extra five dollars? How about the health of the planet and of your fellow human beings? This decision alone can help raise your frequency if that's what you desire.

STEP EIGHT: TAKE ONE RELATIONSHIP HABIT AND UPGRADE IT

What's the first thing that comes to your mind about your

relationships? Think specifically about how you typically express yourself (or don't)—how can you best support yourself to upgrade this pattern?

Take one habit or pattern you notice about yourself and make a declaration that from this moment on, you're choosing something else. For example, if you tend to not accept compliments but instead deflect them or just feel uncomfortable, you could make a declaration: "I, of my own sovereign nature and free will, choose to practice receiving compliments with grace and gratitude from this moment on."

Say this declaration out loud with conviction. Next, write it down. This two-part ritual draws a line in the sand energywise. It instantly shifts you from ignorance to awareness. From now on, that pattern will stand out in your consciousness, supporting you to take action to correct it.

As we talked about in the last chapter, upgrading your frequency in any relationship will shift the relationship itself. Depending on the nature of the relationships you're in, this practice can be either directly supportive immediately, or indirectly supportive down the road. Not everyone wants to get on board with awakening, and it's possible that someone in your life may dig in their heels and say they liked you better the old way. Have the courage of your convictions, and know that what you're doing for your own overall awakening positively affects all beings in the unified field. Even the person objecting to your shift will be positively affected, even though they may not realize it yet.

STEP NINE: SUPPLEMENTS FOR YOUR BODIES

All of your bodies, physical, emotional, mental, and spiritual, can benefit from supplements that support all of the multi-body changes going on during this time. Of course, I'm not a doctor, so check with your health professionals for the most appropriate supplements for you, but I wanted to give you a list of what's worked for me.

- Vegan EPA/DHA—These essential fatty acids are critical when you're moving through the ascension process. I find that taking them within thirty minutes of taking magnesium also is super helpful for brain processes.
- Magnesium—You may notice muscle twitches or sleep challenges as you awaken your third eye, and much of this can be alleviated with magnesium. Magnesium changed my life, and I see deficiency in a huge percentage of clients and students. (Check out Dr. Carolyn Dean's book *The Magnesium Miracle* for some great insight.)
- Electrolytes—This can't be overstated. It's almost as if you're a competitive athlete when you're going through this process, and electrolytes can be easily depleted. Remember that we're dealing with electrical signals throughout all aspects of your bodies, and electrolytes help to facilitate those signals.
- Cell salts—I use a homeopathic version of cell salts, and it helps to balance your energies in a way that I haven't seen with other versions. Cell salts help with overall cell restoration in general, as well. Hyland's homeopathics makes one called Bioplasma (not dairy free). There are multiple dairy-free versions on the market; that's what we use.

YOUR TIMELINE

How you incorporate these different practices depends on who you are. There are some people who operate better in extremes—they'll start a new program on Monday and have completely changed their pattern by Friday. Others need months to integrate just one new change.

The same thing is true about the detox symptoms that accompany this energetic shift. Some people do better by just powering through the detox, not trying to tiptoe around it. Other people operate better by taking one small step at a time, letting it integrate, and then taking the next small step.

You might know yourself well enough to quickly choose the best approach for you. But if not, it's helpful to look back at how you've made changes in the past and follow that pattern.

Take organizing your house. If you decide to declutter, do you work on one drawer each week? Or do you take a week off work to tackle it all at once?

There's no better or worse way, and there's nothing better or worse about shifting quickly or slowly. It's just about knowing yourself and honoring whatever flow you fit in, in order to make your shift sustainable.

The exciting part is that each of these transitions will support the next level of awakening. In other words, the steps get easier as you go. You might start out with one action item a week and find yourself getting so much stronger over the following few weeks that you can add in two or three new actions at the same time.

By the same token, it's important to remember that these shifts can also cause phases of heightened sensitivity. Whether it's feeling sick after eating a specific food that used to never cause you problems or feeling more bothered by a violent TV program or just the sight of two people arguing, it's normal to feel things differently when your higher self is awakened and integrating.

Remember that being more sensitive isn't the same as getting more fragile. The more in tune you are with your natural state, the stronger you are. Honor what feels true for you right now, and relax into the process. As you continue to raise frequency, your strength will grow so that you naturally avoid the things that bother you and attract the things that support you.

A good analogy is the before and after around the dangers of smoking. Before the public realized cigarettes cause cancer, most people were pretty used to the smell of nicotine tar in a room. But once that knowledge became widespread, some people started to really react against it, while others (usually those who still smoked) still didn't mind it.

Much like cigarettes, many people are addicted to lower frequencies. Breaking out of those addictive cycles requires making a shift, and sometimes that shift has to be accompanied by a more intense reaction to really take effect. If you find yourself having trouble breaking free of lower energies and feeling challenged accessing your high-vibe intuitive nature through these steps, visit my website AlyssaMalehorn.com for resources and healing sessions to support your breaking free.

WHAT TO EXPECT

Be aware from the outset that the first three days of making a shift are typically the most challenging. Those first three days are when it's easiest to fall back into old habits and patterns. If that happens, it's important to not judge it. You can simply say, "Okay, there's a part of me that still wants to experience life in the old way," and keep working on raising frequency in other ways. There's nothing wrong with that.

After those first three days, things will likely get a lot easier and more rewarding—you'll feel the beneficial effects of the shift you're making. Then another milestone arrives at around fourteen days. After feeling pretty good for those first few weeks, where your energy is high and you're sleeping better, you may suddenly have a wave of detoxification move through your energy field. Everything from judgment to physical densities starts to purge, coming out through the field as well as through your physical system. You might experience digestive weirdness, crazy dreams, circular thinking, or intense self-judgment.

Usually, any super challenging periods last less than a week—typically three or four days. However, some people might process these shifts in two hours (often with greater intensity of symptoms), while for others, the process might last longer but be a bit less intense. Whether or not you feel symptoms is not an indicator of *whether* you're shifting—it's just a natural outcome from how you individually process energy.

Expect another round of this detoxification about a month later and then another around one year. At that one-year mark, people often start to have intense bursts of low-frequency energy around what they left behind. It might manifest as missing the old patterns—if they decided to move beyond animal products in their diet, they'll start to crave cheese or be distracted by the smell of a barbeque. Conversely, it can manifest as disgust or frustration—for example, if they gave up watching TV, they might have judgment arise against a loved one who still watches TV.

This is all a normal part of the process. What's happening is that you're purging another level of density, and your system is noticing it on the way out. When there's an imbalance, the body's natural reaction is to regain balance by clinging to what's familiar. You're trying to anchor into a lower vibe precisely because you're releasing it.

If you stay the course of coherence—cleaning up your environment and purifying your body—you'll break through this resistance and continue ascending to the next level of frequency. You'll feel amazing there for a while, and then you'll begin breaking through to the next level, which brings another round of resistance. However, subsequent rounds won't feel as low as the previous one did because as you build your energy field and raise frequency, you're "lightening up" in more ways than one. You're bringing more biophotonic energy into your system, which is displacing old patterns and energies. As those old, dense energies get crowded out, they no longer have such a strong foothold.

THE SIGNS OF AWAKENING

As you adjust your diet and stay the course, there are signs of awakening you might experience and should be aware of. Hot flashes, nightmares, chills, and cold and fever symptoms are all common physical side effects during the process of opening up spiritually.

In the spiritually awakening community, we call them "ascension symptoms." Some people tend to glorify these, i.e., subscribing to the belief that some sort of sacrifice or suffering is necessary for progress. That's simply not true—it's just another version of the low-frequency thought pattern/program that nothing good comes without struggle, which we talked about in Chapter 1.

So if your experience of raising consciousness isn't accompanied by discomfort, don't assume that it means you're doing anything wrong or that the changes you've made aren't worthwhile. Again, having symptoms isn't an indicator of spiritual advancement, just a nod to how you personally process and experience energy.

Raising consciousness can also temporarily bring up issues like headaches, joint pain, autoimmune issues, as well as "medical mystery" problems, where some people just can't figure out what's going on. Often these issues recall similar sicknesses you've had as a child—for example, if you had chickenpox as a child, you could have shingles break out as an adult. The same is true of illness that might be within your lineage, but you've never had a problem with it—if asthma runs in your family, you might suddenly come down with bronchitis. Even if there's no specific sickness, you may go through days of unexplained low energy where you just may not feel like getting off the couch.

What's happening is again just a lightening of density. Our souls use the physical body as a way to transmute those energies. Raising your consciousness transforms not only your own issues/distortions but also distortions from your parents, grandparents, and great-grandparents, anything within your DNA is now being hit with the light of awareness.

> Distortion is anything that's not fully aligned with love, sovereignty, and freedom. For a lot of people, 99 percent of their thoughts are distorted. As you start to awaken, you notice those distortions—for example, if you were taking responsibility for someone else's feelings or if you are self-destructive in some way.

Along with changes in your physical body, you may find your emotional energy dipping up and down. Just as your body is detoxifying deeply buried physical issues, raising consciousness brings up long-forgotten emotional experiences for you to process. (Spiritual awakening = emotional clearing. We can't carry emotional baggage and feel free spiritually at the same time.) You might find yourself feeling incredibly happy and upbeat one day, then feeling very down and lethargic the next. Sometimes, you may be hit with waves of grief over something you thought you'd already healed from or regret from the times in your life where you lived within a low-frequency cycle.

At other moments, you might experience bursts of intense energy. For some, this manifests as a panic attack; for others, it compels them to clean their entire house or get super creative.

Your mental energy may fluctuate as well. Some people experience ADD-like symptoms, where they have difficulty focusing; others get hyperfocused on something for a while, throwing their routine out of balance. You might have racing thoughts that keep you up at night. You could also find yourself thinking about your relationships and responsibilities completely differently. Perhaps you suddenly feel less emotionally invested in making others happy while sacrificing yourself, and this leads to a temporary feeling of detachment. You may feel a burning desire to move, quit your job, clear everything out of your life, run away, or generally start life over from scratch.

Finally, you might experience sleep issues during this process. It's common for my students to wake up in the middle of the night at around three or four in the morning and have trouble going back to sleep—it makes perfect sense, as that's the time for the pineal gland to restore itself.

No matter what symptoms you encounter, the application is the same: observation, expression, and compassion. It can be particularly helpful to enlist a compassionate witness, whether a trusted friend or a healer, to help you navigate through the issue in a way that maintains frequency. (This is one of the primary reasons that we created the free Raw Spirituality Community as a support for those undergoing awakening.)

When my partner Zack and I first got together, he started having this weird pain in his leg. It would come and go, and the pain really bothered him when it showed up. I asked him about the first time he remembered having pain there, and he said it came from an injury from many years ago while playing football in high school.

Both of us understood what was happening—our relationship

was bringing more light into his system, and as a result, his body was pushing out the density of that old injury. Along with doing energy work on the injury site and calming the pain with some homeopathy, I asked him to recount exactly what happened for me.

Any pain medications that suppress symptoms just put the issue off until a later date. Homeopathy is a great tool because it works on etheric DNA, so it doesn't interrupt the process of moving something up and out of the system.

Zack remembered that in high school, his state of consciousness was essentially "walk it off." Like most people, he didn't really give himself the love, compassion, and rest he needed—he expected himself to get over things quickly and move on. I asked him to tell me more about his life at that time, and he remembered how devastating the injury was. It happened while he was playing in front of college scouts, and scholarships were in the conversation. Getting injured in front of them was a multifaceted trauma. In addition to the overwhelm and pain of the experience, what he heard afterward was, "Well, your days in football are over. Find something else to do."

After he gave expression to that experience, I empathized and reflected his own emotions back to him: "That must've been so hard—you must have felt so traumatized, so much loss and fear about your future."

He confirmed that yes, he had felt all those things.

It was about giving honor and love to a time that was lacking it. That process jumpstarts the healing process.

JOURNALING

If you don't have a compassionate witness to bring into your healing process, and even if you do, you can experience tremendous healing by writing everything down and being the validating, compassionate witness for yourself. Your body wants to purge the experience out of your system, and external expression can be key to that release.

This is most effective when you write your experience down on paper versus typing it into a phone or computer. What you're trying to do is take something from the unseen world (a thought, a belief, an energy) and put it into a material state. Seeing it manifested on paper, in a physical state external to you, shifts the way the subconscious addresses and heals the issue.

In addition, writing things down activates your brain with your body—you're translating your experience through your eyes, your nervous system, your muscles, and all the oxygen and nutrients flowing through your system to power that motion. This is unbelievably powerful in terms of processing—it takes you from "I don't feel good" to "Now I see clearly." That clarity is the ultimate goal of this detoxification.

We as old souls have our own version of hell, and it's confusion, not pain. That's why writing is one of the best ways to move from confusion to clarity—it allows your unconscious to speak through your hand.

I highly recommend journaling not only in moments of intense shift but throughout your consciousness raising journey. The key is to do it without judgment or even much thought—just let the words flow.

Sometimes, I guide my students to a journaling prompt like, "I reclaim the parts of myself that were fragmented off through trauma or pain. The parts of myself are..."

In response, you can write things like, "The part of myself that felt ashamed," or "The part of myself that felt rushed and hurried all the time," or "The part of myself that felt helpless or hopeless. I reclaim all those parts right now with love." Because our souls may become fragmented through trauma and pain, and we reclaim our lost aspects through love and awareness.

THE INTUITIVE GIFTS

There are eight primary intuitive gifts that are natural for everyone, though we typically each have a few that are more foundational and develop more easily for us. The descriptions in the following sections will help you begin sensing which of these gifts is your strong suit. As you focus more on the gifts you're naturally wired for during this Third Eye Diet process, the other ones will likely begin to emerge and develop as well over time.

CLAIRVOYANCE

Clairvoyance is often thought of as being able to see the future. However, the real definition is more expansive—it refers to perceiving things that are in your mind's eye, almost as though the information is superimposed on the environment. It's not always future facing, though it can be. (This is a subcategory of clairvoyance known as precognition, which is shifted by our free will along with our level of consciousness. This means that anything we perceive in the future can change, based on our own and other's awakening and awareness.)

It's also seeing things multidimensionally. For example, one of my gifts is clairvoyance, and when I look at people, I can choose to see the thought forms around them, their auric energy field or lightbody, as well as any guides or entities that are present around them.

When I close my eyes, I can choose to see places they've been or where they're going, as well as loved ones, traumas, and connections.

I don't do this intentionally unless asked to, to honor privacy and sovereignty in all. The ability to turn your gifts on and off comes with working with an experienced teacher, along with time and practice. Learning to discern what's just your imagination and what's not takes time, practice, and guidance from an experienced teacher. This is primarily because the soul's language *is* your imagination, using your memories, thoughts, and mental imagery to build an intuitive message.

Are you clairvoyant?

- Do visual images stick in your head?
- When you see something, are you able to recall it visually?
- Are you artistic? Do you like to draw?
- Do you like to take photos?
- Are you someone who gets an image about things that will happen in the future?
- Do you get an image in your mind's eye very easily when someone describes something to you?
- Are you really drawn to color?

CLAIRAUDIENCE

People who are clairaudient many times think they're imagining things because they perceive information through their auditory means. Sometimes, it's like someone's speaking in your ear or in the room, while at other times, it's a voice in your head that often sounds like your own. My whole life I've heard what I call the "cocktail party noise," which sounds like lots of people talking and clinking glasses, with laughter and music. This is an aspect of clairaudience, specifically hearing through multiple astral realms.

Are you clairaudient?

- Do songs or snippets of songs pop into your head with no warning and then repeat or get "stuck"? (Many times, there is a message in the lyrics from your guides or departed loved ones.)
- Have you ever heard your name called when no one was home? (This is mediumship clairaudience, where those on the other side are speaking.)
- Do you sometimes hear your own voice in your head, but it comes through with an unfamiliar thought, solution, or strategy?
- Are you more comfortable having music or television on most of the time for background noise?
- Would you rather talk on the phone instead of text or email, even if you only have one sentence to say?

CLAIRCOGNIZANCE

This is simply intrinsic knowledge—you just know something, and no one can talk you out of it. There might not be clear logic behind it, and it might not make any sense, but it's trustworthy because you've received the information from the unified field.

Are you claircognizant?

- Do you sometimes just know something with no reason or justification for knowing it?
- Are you an avid learner, an intellectual, or a reader?
- Do you love documentaries and anything educational?
- If you're going to read something, is it typically nonfiction?
- When you have a sense of knowing, do you feel it in your brain, as though it's something you learned, even when it's new, intuitive information?

CLAIRSENTIENCE + EMPATHIC ABILITY

People often mistake clairsentience as claircognizance. But where claircognizance is a mental knowing, clairsentience is when you receive psychic information through the body, emotions, and feelings. You feel an emotion, like love or fear, that you've picked up from others or the collective consciousness. It might manifest in your physical body as an adrenaline rush or fatigue. Understandably, this can be a big reason for feeling overwhelmed by the collective consciousness.

Those of us who are clairsentient are also typically highly empathic, feeling others' feelings, sometimes to an intense degree. While there are some super high-vibe aspects of this, heart coherence helps tremendously with the less helpful, low-vibe effects of this trait.

Are you clairsentient and empathic?

- Do you tend to feel others' feelings?
- Do you often take on others' problems, move into over-compassion, or feel overly responsible for how others feel?
- Are boundaries an issue for you? Codependency?
- Do you feel overwhelmed pretty regularly?
- Have you ever felt a pain in your physical body when you were around someone who was ill, and the pain dissipated when you left?

CLAIRGUSTANCE + CLAIRALIENCE

Clairgustance is tasting something in your mouth that's not there. You might taste a penny or a mint, but there will be nothing physically there.

Clairalience is the same, only related to the olfactory sense—smelling something that isn't there in the physical world but that exists in the astral. Smelling a loved one's perfume after they've made their transition is one common example of this. I used to smell cigarette smoke every time my deceased aunt was around. It was like my whole car was filled with it, and it wouldn't subside until I spoke to her, acknowledging she was there.

Both clairsentience and clairgustance tend to connect to mediumship. When we tend to tap into these gifts, it's because a loved one on the other side is coming through with tastes and smells to say hi and let you know they're still around. This is more prevalent when we're really feeling alone and a loved one is able to reassure us. (Not all loved ones on the other side are in a position to come through in this way.) When my Aunt Nell was still in physical form, she would always make chicken and dumplings for every special occasion or holiday. So when she was around in spirit, I would suddenly have the taste of dumplings in my mouth, because as a kid, I loved holidays visiting with her.

Are you clairgustant or clairalient?

- Are you a foodie? Do you love experimenting with new recipes, tastes, and textures?
- Are you very sensitive to smells?
- Are you someone who can think of a chocolate cake you had, and your mouth will start to water? Can you truly remember it, drawing up all the complexities of whatever it was that you ate? When someone else says, "That was really good," do you say, "Oh my God, it had hints of smokiness!"
- When you think of departed loved ones, do you tend to smell their perfume, flowers, smoke, or food?
- Do you get tastes in your mouth or smells in the room when you're meditating?

PSYCHOMETRY

This gift refers to touching an object or person and feeling its energy. Back when I worked as a massage therapist, I could tell a lot about a client as soon as I put my hands on them. Did they have out-of-control cancer cells? Were they cheating on their spouse? Did they have an infection of some type? Were they repressing fear?

Early in my professional life, I really struggled with feeling as though I was invading people's privacy, so I created a contract with my highest self and my guides to only perceive what would be in my clients' and my highest good, without anything else coming through. Since all living beings put all their information into the field, nothing is truly private, but I only chose to access the information that was beneficial and appropriate to allowing me to support them in the most benevolent way.

This modality is how some people use their intuitive gifts to find missing people. If you hand me someone's keys, for instance, I can likely tell you where that person is, where they've recently been or where they often go. Finding missing people is extremely challenging emotionally for me personally, so I don't typically do this type of work. It can be especially overwhelming to locate someone's physical body, know that their soul/spirit is no longer with that body, and as an empath, feel all of the feelings of the deceased *and* the family members left behind. Those who are well suited for this type of work are great with psychometry but not as developed with clairsentience and empathic ability.

SOME INTUITIVE DEVELOPMENT EXERCISES TO SUPPORT YOU IN THE PROCESS

Everyone's third eye awakens differently. We all have natural inclinations toward different avenues. For instance, someone who's very visual in life tends to see images in their mind's eye as their intuition is awakening. They often chalk it up to their imagination, but it's really their higher self speaking through their most open channel. Someone else who is a highly verbal processor, or really connects with music, might hear songs repeating in their head or hear sounds in nature with unusual clarity.

Someone who's very kinesthetic will be clairsentient, where

you have clear emotional feelings. Sometimes, you have feelings in your physical body; like, perhaps you won't understand why your heart suddenly starts racing. That's because you're clairsentient and there's something sparking energy in your field that you're reacting to.

This can be challenging. Like coming out of a dark room into the sunlight hurts your eyes for a while, this sudden ability to perceive new-to-you information in the field can be overwhelming, especially when you're tuning into a lot of sad or painful information.

One of my students who lives in El Paso, Texas, told me that the night before the 2019 El Paso shooting, she woke up in the middle of the night with a racing heart. She went to check on her kids without any idea why, and she slept on their floor that night.

"I just couldn't leave them," she said. "I was so mama bear protective. My heart was racing, like I was having a panic attack."

She realized later that she was feeling that energy in the field through precognition and clairsentience.

Why would we have access to this information sometimes and not all the time?

Even intuitive awakening is a tool for detoxifying low frequencies, allowing you to heal. I asked my student what that experience reminded her of, and she said that it took her back to having lost a child many years ago. She picked up on the particular energy of the violence coming to her area because her body was ready to heal from that long-ago grief.

There's always a big-picture reason that we intuitively pick up on things. We don't just enhance our intuition and spiritual ascension so we can make more money or know what someone thinks about us, or even so we can be in service in the intuitive arts. We do it because every bit of knowledge, feeling, or information that comes through the field is ultimately for our own healing, which then brings us into a higher level of service. My student is now able to be so much more in service to her kids after having resolved the grief around the one she lost. She'll be more present, less of a fearful mother, and she'll allow herself and them more freedom.

NATURAL ENERGY HEALERS

The manipulation of energy happens all the time. It's just typically used in ways that aren't for healing. It's natural for everyone to use their energy not just to perceive what's happening in someone's field but to actually affect it. When it's done with the intention of healing or helping, it's known as lightwork, energy work, or energy medicine.

Growing up, people would often say they felt better around me because I exuded a natural healing energy. Just by being present, I naturally helped them shift and balance energies. When I focused on it, pretty amazing things happened.

When I was about fifteen years old, I was at a festival with some friends when we met a group of boys from England. As we were walking around the festival grounds, one of them said he had a migraine and headed back to the parking lot. When we found him, he was sitting on the tailgate of his truck, crying and holding his head.

I asked him, "Can I put my hands on your head?"

He just nodded, unable to speak because of the pain.

I put my hands on his head and felt a flood of compassion for this guy. I had migraines from the time I was thirteen, so I completely understood how much pain he was in and piled on the compassion and love.

Suddenly, he looked up at me, got off the tailgate, and began moving his neck around. Then he got down on one knee and asked me to marry him.

I remember laughing, feeling happy but a little embarrassed. Later, I went to my aunt's house. She was psychic as well and helped to support me in my awakening. (Although helpful and super supportive, she certainly didn't have a well-thought-out plan for that—but that's a whole different book!) I asked her what had happened, and she said, "Your love and compassion for him changed what was happening in his body. It's as simple as that."

I've been teaching energy healing and mentoring students for over twenty-five years, and it's still that simple. There are lots of different attunements (activations) you can receive to boost your healing ability, and there are modalities and techniques you can learn that can accelerate and amplify your healing work. And truly one of my favorite things to do is guide, mentor, and attune students to Channeled Light Healing™ energy (multidimensional energy spiritual awakening/healing modality). That said, the bottom line is that we all naturally have the power to shift energy through love. When you move through the processes in this book, you're going to develop and awaken your third eye and notice some natural activations in how you heal yourself. This will extend to your healing impact on others, whether you seek training and attunements or just allow love and compassion to grow and expand with your focus.

As you begin to discover your natural intuitive gifts, moving into a coherent state will help support both the unfolding of the gifts and your overall awakening/healing. Being part of a community of people who are in the same process can be the most supportive of all.

CONCLUSION

As a child grows older and bigger, they experience what we call "growing pains." Because parents know to expect these discomforts as part of the growing process, they can offer the child reassurance and even teach the child to comfort themselves.

But once we become an adult, we seem to expect ourselves to have everything figured out. At that point, disruptions to the status quo suddenly seem alarming to people. We tell ourselves that everything is stable by this time, but it's really just a story we tell ourselves to create the stability we crave.

The natural state of all living things is evolution and expansion. But expansion is accompanied by disruption, i.e., a change in what used to feel stable. This is true of spiritual expansion, physical growth, family systems, friendships, and romantic relationships, even the marketplace.

The mission of this book is to support you in your evolutionary journey to spiritual awakening by offering a transmitting resonance combined with tools that raise frequency and show you how to use them in the most efficient way. At first, using these tools may cause disruption and even discomfort, but even those disruptions are just part of reestablishing flow in your life.

When you turn on a hose or a faucet that hasn't run in many years, the water comes out in big, messy bursts at first. Before long, though, it begins to flow cleanly and smoothly. We have a tendency to glorify the flow state, without recognizing that establishing it in the first place necessarily brings stops and starts. But these disruptions are as natural as the state of flow itself.

YOUR THIRD EYE DIET

The Third Eye Diet adds up to more than the sum of its parts. Every area of your life—what you eat, drink, breathe, think, feel, share, and respond to—contributes to your over-all awakening. When you give even a tiny bit of attention to one aspect of your diet, you give yourself the gift of raised consciousness. Each baby step builds a new level of trust between the different aspects of yourself.

If you're wondering where to start, or how much to start with, do as much as you feel drawn to. Whatever you select is the perfect amount for you—there's no too little or too much. I honor your desire to expand your level of awareness, your con-sciousness, and your sense of oneness, and I honor your pace.

I'm incredibly excited for your journey. Spiritual activation (spiritual awakening/ascension) is the natural evolutionary process that exists as an umbrella over different aspects of intuition.

When you start to raise frequency, your heart center opens, and you feel a connection to your highest self. At the same time, you notice all the energies around you in a different way. But because your center doesn't have wisdom yet, you can have trigger reactions to this influx. Your new state can bring a hypersensitivity to what is going wrong with the world, and you might form judgments as a self-protective excuse to withdraw from others.

It's important to remember that as multidimensional beings, we bounce among different levels of perception, depending on what we're going through and what part of our lives we're referring to. I may have a really high level of frequency when it comes to playing with my dog, but if he turns around and bites me, I'll go into a lower frequency and want to dominate him out of a survival instinct. You may feel a high level of consciousness when it comes to your romantic relationship, but as soon as you enter a room full of family members, everything triggers you.

As Ram Dass said in one of his many talks, "If you think you're enlightened, go spend a week with your family."

But as you maintain your Third Eye Diet, you'll stop swinging back and forth between your head and your heart, judgment and generosity. Over time, you'll feel your own and everyone else's sovereignty. You'll develop the wisdom that having an open heart all the time doesn't make you vulnerable—it makes you strong.

As your strength grows to support your newly raised frequency, you won't feel as easily influenced by the material world or lower frequencies. You also won't have to put as much conscious effort into your new practices. You may still want to do the rituals because you enjoy them, but not because you're desperately trying to keep yourself feeling good. Your life becomes one holistic ritual, an ongoing meditation.

You begin to live so much more in the now, no longer thinking of past regrets or how others wronged you, or feeling uncertainty about the future. There's an acceptance that all is well. Even when you desire to improve something, you understand that what you're in now is perfect for now. You feel more and more balanced.

It's important to understand all of this as part of a natural process. As we move through it, we must cultivate ease and gentleness with ourselves and honor for everyone on the earth plane. Every being goes through this at some point in this life or another. Because of that, no one can be ahead or behind on the journey. We're all individualized aspects of the divine, with our own unique journey. The path to higher consciousness will generally follow the template I've described here, but everyone will experience it in their own way. All we can do is be supportive of ourselves and each other, as much as we can be.

No matter what you choose to integrate from this book, you'll find it incredibly empowering. Instead of moving through life asleep at the wheel, you're taking charge of your experience. Eventually, this empowerment will reveal more of how you're designed to uniquely serve the world.

WHAT TO DO LATER

As we said earlier, there's no pinnacle to reach on this journey. So when your journey leads you to a place where you feel wonderfully spiritually awakened and your intuition is off the charts, it's a great time to examine what drew you to this journey in the first place.

QUESTIONS TO ASK YOURSELF

- Why do I even care about being spiritually awake?
- What benefit am I providing to myself by being in this state now? What benefit am I providing to others by being in this state now?
- How does everything I'm doing allow me to be in service to others? To myself? To the planet?
- What do I feel like I'll "fix" by doing this? Do I not want to be fearful anymore? Is it because I want to feel special by having something that other people don't have?

There are no right or wrong answers. Being honest with yourself will help awaken another level of awareness. Remember, there's always a new level to ascend to. At first, you may not feel like you want to question your new state too much. But whether you do it on your own or wait for an event in your life to provoke it, your newly awakened consciousness will always draw you to opportunities for more healing and raising frequency.

You'll also find yourself experiencing your life with new consciousness. Things will happen, and you'll ask yourself, "What am I supposed to learn from this?" Maybe you keep finding yourself in relationships in the same pattern or responding to events in your work life according to an old program.

My book *How Old Is Your Soul?* really goes into how to heal these issues on different levels. When we know where we are in terms of our own soul age and where the people in our lives are based on their soul age, that understanding helps so much to bring compassion and awareness to those relationships rather than judgment and frustration (with ourselves or with someone else). Higher awareness yields gentleness, patience, and kindness around the stuff we're working through.

It's beautiful to reach a point where you're eager to learn the lesson so you don't have to repeat it. But eventually, you come to realize there might be nothing to figure out. *What if the only lesson is to learn how to be in a coherent state of love?* When you approach your awakening process from that perspective, you can observe the patterns and programs in your mind and heal them without the pressure to figure it out and heal it once and for all. Instead of trying to get to the bottom of your issues, discovering low frequencies starts to feel as natural as bubbles floating up to the surface.

HEART CHANGES

When you move through this process, your concept of vulnerability will also shift. Before you started, you had a set of patterns that kept you feeling relatively secure—if someone were to criticize you, you might have gone into defensive mode or perhaps protected yourself through constant remorse and apologizing. But the more you move through the awakening process, the more you see vulnerability as a strength. If someone criticizes you, you can trust that there's a purpose in that interaction, even if you're not aware of what it is. You feel a sense of sovereignty over how much those events disturb your peace or not. You're no longer at the mercy of your emotions or anyone else's.

Every emotion has its purpose, even anger. It's not about being so blissed out all the time that you don't feel anything. Rather, it's about having feelings but not being attached to the stories around them. If you say something that doesn't feel good to me, I can feel emotions without creating a story that you're a bad person or that I'm being victimized. You can let yourself feel the emotions, allow them to move through you, and shift back into a coherent state. That's when you allow the moments of clarity and healing to flow, and you'll have higher-level awareness: Why did that feel the way it felt? Am I resisting something, or am I willing to meet that feeling with coherent love?

It's such a relief because you realize that your projections onto other people and yourself have been just that: projections. The story might have a basis in fact, and it's totally valid for you to refuse to let that story play out in your life again. *But as you move into self-authority, you become the author of your own story.* There's such a freedom in that, and it feels wonderful.

This sovereignty helps shift the tendency to compare yourself with others who are on the same spiritual path. You might have embarked on this path thinking it would make you finally feel good enough. But by staying on this path, you'll come to realize that you always were. Bumping yourself out of an old pattern feels like creating something new in your life, but it's not really new—it's simply removing the blocks that were in the way of what you always had inside you.

This provides security when you find differences within the community of other spiritually awakened people. What feels resonant to you may not feel resonant to everyone else and vice versa. It's okay if the collective truth might not agree with you. Standing in your own sovereignty within this situation can require a certain amount of courage at first, especially if the awakened community is your main support.

That's why, when people join our Raw Spirituality Community, I encourage them to share their heart and ask questions. We're all walking through this process together as an ascending soul family, and it's more than okay for us to experience it differently.

If you'd like to continue learning or interacting with me, I'd love to see you in our Raw Spirituality Community at RawSpirituality.com. There are free courses and paid ones. There are groups, and you can connect with the commUNITY.

You're also welcome to head over to our podcast, Raw Spirituality, which is available wherever you listen to podcasts. Zack and I, as spiritual catalysts, talk about all of this stuff. People who are in the Raw Spirituality Community can suggest topics for the podcast, as well as ask questions and connect with others in our listener family.

You may be interested in some of the groups within the community, where we have more deep-dive lessons into spiritual awakening and the ascension process, as well as live events held online, so you can attend them no matter where you live.

I'd also love to invite you to go to my website and see what other events and healing tools may be supportive for you, and so we can get to know each other. You'll find me at AlyssaMalehorn.com.

As we're talking about community, I'd love to invite you to participate in our Raw Spirituality Community. It's truly a beautiful gathering place that offers an opportunity to connect with others who are moving through an awakening process in all different levels, all different ways, all over the world. We offer a podcast where we discuss topics you suggest, as well as courses in awakening, expansion, healing, and multidimensional living, and private groups where you can access things like bonus podcast episodes and live online events that people attend from all over the world.

WHAT DOES LIVING A MORE INTUITIVE, SPIRITUALLY ACTIVATED LIFE REALLY MEAN?

Even as you know that there's no pinnacle of this awakening process, you might wonder where it's leading—what does living a more activated life really look like?

Even with all the changes you might make in your diet (the food you consume, the media you watch, the way you take care of your environment, how you are in relationships, etc.), living an awakened life looks very much the same as it did before. The biggest difference is in how you feel and your perception—primarily, there's a sense of coming home to yourself. You have fewer and fewer feelings of self-betrayal, feeling disconnected, making decisions that don't align with your highest self. You stop worrying about making mistakes—instead of looking for what went wrong, you see everything as simply experience. Life feels easier and clearer—there's an ability to prioritize what really feels true for you and a natural courage that supports you even when your choices seem unpopular amongst the people in your world. No matter who is with you or not, you feel supported by your highest self, your divine team, and the overall process of life. The pressure of daily life goes away and yields to the buoyancy and gratitude/coherence of simply being alive.

The way humans are wired is funny. We're wired to create a challenge for growth, and eventually, as we move through this process, we no longer create constriction in an effort to have expansion. The human way, meaning the lower vibratory way, is like a chick breaking out of an egg. It's like you have to have this barrier to break through to prove you're developed enough. You're strong enough to do it. But eventually, you don't need the egg anymore to push you through the struggle. When you reach a point where you're simply ready to give that struggle up, you find that the knowledge you wanted was always there—the difference is that you're now ready to act on it. You realize that you can move into a coherent state and just breathe and see what shows up for you.

I'd like to say how much I deeply appreciate your contribution to the unified field—your curiosity, your willingness to learn, the self-love that led you to this book, your openness to concepts or tools that you might not have been open to in the past. We all support each other with what we contribute with all of our thoughts, with every moment we spend in a coherent state, and with every moment we spend in meditation, just being.

I love you. I honor your being, always in all ways. Thank you.

—ALYSSA

ACKNOWLEDGMENTS

From my heart, a huge thank you to my clients, students, and our Raw Spirituality Community for inspiring this book.

Thank you, Chelsea Batten, for your skill, curiosity, and patience as we worked through the organization and seemingly endless details!

Mama and Daddy, thank you, thank you, thank you.

Finally, to my partner in all things, Zack, and my most precious gift, Wolf: my deepest gratitude and love. Your encouragement and support has made this and everything else possible.

RESOURCES

CHAPTER 1

LEARNING THE SCIENCE BEHIND SPIRITUALITY

Dr. Joe Dispenza is a leading researcher and educator on the processes that accompany third eye awakening. If you're interested in exploring this interesting topic, the following books by Dr. Dispenza are a great place to start.:

- *You Are the Placebo*
- *Breaking the Habit of Being Yourself*
- *Becoming Supernatural*

CHAPTER 3

ZACK'S "HOLY CACAO!"

- Approximately 1½ to 2 cups almond milk or other plant-based milk, either cold or heated (You can also make raw almond milk by blending 1 heaping tbsp raw almond butter with 1½ cups spring water.)
- 1 tsp vanilla extract
- Dash sea salt

- Approx. 1½ tbsp raw organic cacao powder (We use Essential Living or Navitas brands.)
- Approx. 2 pitted Medjool dates, depending on sweetness level desired (If you're not using a high-powered blender, substitute 1 tbsp maple syrup.)
- 1 large tbsp raw almond butter (Other nut butters can be substituted, especially if you're using a different type of plant milk. For example, cashew butter would be good with cashew milk, hazelnut butter with hazelnut milk, etc. You can even use cocoa butter if you want an extra rich cocoa flavor. For all of our nut/seed butters, we like Artisana or ChocolaTree brands.)
- Optional: 1 tbsp Lairds Superfood Creamer, unsweetened

Put all ingredients in a high-powered blender and blend on high until smooth and frothy. Enjoy!

CHAPTER 4
RAISING COHERENCE

To join with a worldwide community of people on the journey to raising coherence, visit the HeartMath Global Coherence Initiative (HeartMath.org/gci/).

COHERENCE MONITOR

You can obtain your own coherence monitor at AlyssaMalehorn.com/shop.

THIRD EYE DIET STEP-BY-STEP COHERENCE EXERCISE

1. Focus on the area in the center of your chest.

2. Slow down your breathing.
3. Imagine or intend that you're breathing in and out of the heart center.
4. Breathe in your chosen word/feeling, letting it fill your chest.
5. Exhale the chosen word/feeling, letting it fill your body and then expand out into the field around you.
6. Repeat, while allowing the feeling to expand with every breath. Build the energy and continue as long as you can sustain the feeling.

INNER-EASE™ TECHNIQUE FROM HEARTMATH INSTITUTE

This is another exercise that accomplishes the same goal as the Coherence exercise in the previous section, but it uses different steps to offer a quick approach for moments when you're triggered or knocked out of balance while at work, in public, or in the midst of a conflict with another person.

1. When you are stressed, acknowledge your feelings.
2. Take a short time-out to do Heart-Focused Breathing.
3. Imagine with each breath that you are drawing in a feeling of inner ease.
4. When the stressful feelings have calmed, affirm with a heartfelt commitment that you want to anchor and maintain the state of ease throughout your projects, challenges, and daily interactions.

CHAPTER 5
LEARNING ABOUT PLANT-BASED EATING

Find a full list of Earthling Ed's resources on plant-based

eating (including his 2017 documentary *Land of Hope and Glory*, video library, TEDx presentations, *The Disclosure* podcast, and his restaurant Unity Diner) at his website, EarthlingEd.org/.

CHAPTER 6
FOCUSED LIFE FORCE ENERGY

As mentioned throughout this book, using FLFE made an extraordinary difference in our lives. We immediately noticed easier, deeper meditation, overall uplifting feelings, support for physical and emotional healing, and a whole lot more. You can find some of the company's 5G studies and other research on their site FLFE.net/alyssa. You can also watch interviews of me with the founders of FLFE on my website, AlyssaMalehorn.com.

And, of course, sign up for your free fifteen-day trial of the FLFE service at FLFE.net/alyssa, or use the QR code here.

SOUND ENERGY

The Humming Effect by Andi and Jonathan Goldman offers deeper insight into how a simple sound can wake up internal energies that help with the awakening process.

For more about the *Sa Ta Na Ma* singing meditation,

including a guide to practicing it yourself, visit AlzheimersPrevention.org/research/kirtan-kriya-yoga-exercise/.

PERSONAL CARE RESOURCES

Uninformed Consent: The Hidden Dangers in Dental Care by Hal Huggins and Thomas E. Levy provides a window into the effect of metals on our overall health.

The Environmental Working Group's online database, Skin Deep, gives toxicity scores for thousands of household and personal products. Find it at EWG.org/skindeep/.

Use the QR code here for a special price on my favorite super high-quality essential oils.

CHAPTER 9

GOLDEN MILK

This traditional Ayurvedic recipe is a delicious way to consume high-vibe ingredients that support your third eye awakening. It's creamy, comforting, and takes just five minutes to prepare!

- 1½ cups light coconut milk (canned is best)
- 1½ cups unsweetened plain almond milk
- 1½ tsp ground turmeric

- ¼ tsp ground ginger
- 1 tbsp coconut oil
- 1 pinch ground black pepper
- Your favorite sweetener (we like maple syrup, date syrup, pure stevia, or pure monk fruit)

Combine coconut milk, almond milk, ground turmeric, ground ginger, coconut oil, black pepper, and sweetener in a small saucepan. Whisk to combine and warm over medium heat for about four minutes, while whisking, until golden milk is hot to the touch but not boiling. Turn off heat and taste to adjust flavor. Add more sweetener to taste, or more turmeric/ginger for intense spice.

ABOUT THE AUTHOR

ALYSSA MALEHORN has been an intuitive channel her entire life. Learning how to function with that level of sensitivity taught her how to thrive in the physical world while living multidimensionally. Now, Alyssa serves as a spiritual teacher and ascension guide who supports higher-consciousness awakening in others through live events, retreats, courses, and coaching. She is the creator of Channeled Light Healing—an ever-expanding energy healing modality that is twenty-five years in the making—and a mentor for others in the holistic, healing, and intuitive arts. She is the cohost of the *Raw Spirituality Podcast* and author of the book *How Old Is Your Soul?*

CPSIA information can be obtained
at www.ICGtesting.com
Printed in the USA
FSHW010725020421
80003FS